A Collector's
Guide to Nineteenth-Century
Jugs

Volume II

KATHY HUGHES

Very Best Wishes,

Kathy Hughes

Taylor Publishing Company
Dallas, Texas

Library of Congress Number: 85-2227

ISBN 0-87833-036-4

Book design: Margaret F. Kemp

Printed in U.S.A. by
Taylor Publishing Company
Dallas, Texas

Contents

Preface

When I first started working on my book, A Collector's Guide to Nineteenth Century Jugs, there had been nothing definitive written on the subject. Since that time two books have been published, and to the delight of established collectors, interest has grown by leaps and bounds both on the part of new collectors and of dealers. My first book was a digest of 200 patterns of jugs designed to help individuals to identify pieces which they owned. This second book is a continuation of that digest illustrating with pictures of actual pieces another 232 patterns. In addition, this book contains a section, which is most informative of 108 pictures taken from the Registration Books in the Public Records Office in London, England. Examples of these jugs have not come to my hand personally, but the reader may have in his possession examples of them. Thus, these two sections of this book will help with identification and dating of another 340 designs of relief moulded jugs. I hope that you will find it helpful and informative.

Kathy Hughes

Acknowledgements

In addition to the many people who helped me in compiling my first book, I would like to add the names of Mr. Cameron Hall, Mr. W.J. Rees, Mr. Bruce Leys, Mrs. A.A. Love, Mrs. Barbara Anderson, Mrs. Hermone Spence, Mrs. Paul Tucker and Blair Rice, Professional Photographer who have all added bits and pieces to the knowledge of 19th century jugs through their collections and their interest.

Digest of jugs

1
Pratt Type Jug
Unknown
c. 1790

A blue and white version of Hughes jug number 2, Book 1.

Height: 6 inches
Unmarked

2
Putti and Spear
Spode
c. 1800

A glazed cane coloured jug which has been thrown and sprigged. This stone-ware jug bears a putto with a spear being carried by two others on one side and two putti with spears resting under a tree on the reverse. A hops vine surrounds the neck and goes down the handle.

Height: Unknown
Unmarked
From the Morpeth Collection

3
Cupids at Play
Turner
c. 1800 (1795-1805)

A fine buff coloured porcelaneous stoneware jug which has been thrown and sprigged. Under the brown rim, is a border of grapevines sheltering three

1

playful cupids. There is an engine turned border at the foot.

Height: 5 inches
Impressed: **Turner**

Height: 9½ inches
Impressed: **Adams**
From the John and Linda Dohmlo Collection

5
Quatrefoil and Holly
Wedgwood
c. 1810

A saltglaze stoneware body with a quatrefoil border and a holly leaves border surrounding the bowl. An applied border of lavender leaves surrounds the top and bottom. This is a good example of wares showing the transition from jugs thrown with applied decoration to the totally moulded jugs of the 19th century.

Height: 5⅞ inches
Impressed: **Wedgwood**
From the Cameron Hall Collection

4
Classical
Adams
c. 1802

A medium blue jasper dip jug which has been thrown and sprigged, with white classical figures standing in marble column niches. A ring of fuchsias hang from the arches, grape leaves surround the neck, and vines decorate the handle. The silver top is hallmarked with an indistinct date which appears to be 1802, but cannot be later than 1805.

6
Peace and Plenty
Unknown
c. 1810

A glazed cane coloured jug made of stoneware which features a classical figure representing Peace with an olive branch on one side, and one represent-

ing Plenty bearing flowers and fruit on the reverse. These figures sit under a large arch outlined with alternating rosettes and leaves. The bottom is ringed with a row of acanthus leaf tops, the neck with barley leaf tops.

Height: Unknown
Unmarked
From the Morpeth Collection

7
Bouquet
Unknown
c. 1816

A highly glazed earthenware jug with six panels, each containing a long spray of various multi-coloured flowers.

Diagonal screening at the top is outlined underglaze in aqua. The handle is bright aqua.

Height: 6½ inches
Unmarked

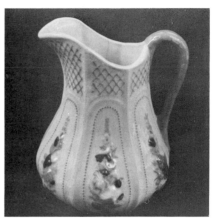

8
"The Snuff Taker" Toby Jug
Unknown
c. 1820

A tan stoneware jug with metal lid in the shape of the Georgian Toby Jug

called "The Snuff Taker." The entire bowl of the jug is in the shape of a tubby little eighteenth century gentleman in waistcoat and tri-corner hat. In his hand he holds a snuff pot from which he is getting ready to take a sniff. The smile on his face displays the joy of his anticipation while he stands in a bunch of grape vines.

Height: 6½ inches
Unmarked

9
The Kill
J.D. Bagster
c. 1825

A tan stoneware jug seemingly identical to the Phillips and Bagster example, Hughes jug number 10, Book 1. This time the collar is marked J.D. Bagster instead of Phillips and Bagster.

Height: 6 inches
Impressed: **J.D. Bagster** on the dog collar
From the W.J. Rees Collection

10
Bouquet
Probably H. & R. Daniels
c. 1825

A glazed white porcelaine jug with embossed lavender flowers around the bowl and hop vines around the neck. There is a band of lavender beading around the foot, a gilded band around the neck and an angular handle.

Height: 6¼ inches
Unmarked

11
Bouquet
William Ridgway
c. 1825

A white stoneware jug with a band of blue flowers around the neck and a cluster of assorted flowers on each side and on the front. There is a fierce bearded mask with a large ring in his mouth for a spout. This jug is much like Bouquet A and B, but it is much lower and more bulbous. While the flowers appear to be the same, these are

arranged differently from those on the other two jugs.

Height: 4½ inches
Embossed: The newly discovered Ridgway mark with the pattern number 438 inside.

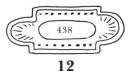

12
The Sacrifice

Possibly Adams
c. 1830

A low white stoneware jug with a dark blue band at the neck and halfway down the handle. It has been thrown, then sprigged with classical figures. An eagle and an angel are at the spout, a girl worshipping at an altar watched by a dog on one side, and two women offering a sacrifice on the reverse.

Height: 3 inches
Unmarked

13
Bird and Butterfly

Minton
c. 1830

A lovely brown and white stoneware jug with a bird looking at a butterfly on a tree branch among flowers and leaves. These are sprigged while around the base of the neck is a press moulded diaper pattern with 4 petal flowers inside the diamonds.

Height: 6 inches
Impressed in a lozenge: Godden's Minton mark no. 2690, with pattern No. 14 impressed within.
Courtesy of the Minton Museum

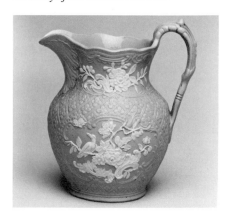

14
Boar's Head
Schidler and Gerbing
c. 1830

Hanging game very similar to those on Hughes jug no. 6 7a, Book 1 have been placed on a German terracotta coloured stoneware body. The most inter-

esting feature of the jug is a large boar's head which serves as a spout.

Height: 7¼ inches
Impressed: **S. & G.**
Impressed: **18**

15
Wild Boar and Deer
Schidler and Gerbing
c. 1830

A jug very similar in shape and design to Hughes jug no. 12, Book 1, Resting Deer. This, however, was produced by the German firm, Schidler and Gerbing, in green glazed red stoneware with four deer among foliage on one side and three wild boar on the reverse. On the front of the jug is a little rabbit at a fence.

Height: 4½ inches
Incised: **S. & G.**
Incised: **11**

16
Acanthus and Bluebells
Unknown
c. 1830

A brightly glazed white stoneware jug with a bright pink background. Acanthus leaves alternate with bluebell stalks around the bowl. Hop vines

encircle the neck. Dudson used this motif extensively in the 1860's.

Height: 7¾ inches
Unmarked
From the Cameron Hall Collection

17
Classical
Unknown
c. 1830

A highly glazed porcelaine jug with lavender-blue ground and white sprigged classical figures. On the front of the jug sit two birds on the edge of a large white bowl placed on a table. A snake body forms the handle and surrounds the neck. The head with open mouth makes a spout and looks more like the head of a bird than a snake. (Compare to Hughes jug number 13, Book 1, Hunt Jug).

6

Height: 4 inches
Unmarked

18
Mother and Baby

Unknown
c. 1830

A white stoneware jug with blue ground which has been thrown then sprigged with a cow and a calf on one side and a horse with her foal on the reverse. There is a white engine-turned border at the base and a small foot-rim.

Height: 2¾ inches
Unmarked

19
Surprise, Mirth and Disgust

Unknown
c. 1830

A very humorous design on a grey stoneware jug heavily decorated with figures in deep relief. The full figures of a man and wife stand with very disgusted looks on their faces as they stare at the rear end of a donkey which is holding a man and child. These last two have looks of total disbelief. One other rotund figure holds his sides in uncontrollable laughter. What could have happened? This theme is repeated on the reverse but with the addition of a

wigged male head whose features also show complete amusement.

Height: 10½ inches
Unmarked
From the Cliborne Collection.

20
MacBeth

Unknown
c. 1830

A very fine textured cream coloured stoneware jug with dark brown medallions containing the figures of Mac-Beth, a reclining stag and a figure of a Muse. There is engine turning on the bottom. The quality of the ceramic body puts one in mind of Turner or Wedgwood.

Height: 6½ inches
Unmarked

A multi-colour stoneware jug trimmed with pink lustre. On each side a winged lion stands on his hind feet among vines and flowers. There is a band of foliage around the neck and pink lustre rings around the bottom.

Height: 5¾
Unmarked

22
Bundle of Faggots

Ridgway & Co.
October 1, 1835

This green stoneware Ridgway version of the Bundle of Faggots design was registered under the same mark and date as the earlier Tam O'Shanter and Linen Fold jugs. This piece has a tankard shape with a bundle of bamboo surrounding it. As the tankard design was registered by T & R Boote in 1842, it is likely that the early Tam O'Shanter mark was used on a later jug.

Height: 8 inches
Impressed:
**Published by
Wm. Ridgway & Co.
Hanley
October 1, 1835**

21
Winged Lion

Unknown
c. 1830

23
Floral Ring

William Ridgway & Co.
October 1, 1835

Another enamelled and highly glazed stoneware jug registered under the same number as Ridgway's Tam O'Shanter jug. (See Hughes no. 27 Book 1.) This example is tan with a ring of multi-coloured enameled flowers around the bowl.

Height: 6¾ inches
Impressed:
Published by
W. Ridgway & Co.
Hanley
October 1, 1835
Impressed: **12**
Painted in red: 906

24
Floral

Perhaps Wm. Hackwood *
c. 1835

A light Staffordshire blue earthenware jug of hexagonal shape. Six cartouches containing sprays of various flowers surround the bowl, and six cartouches containing apple blossom sprays surround the neck. There is a high foliage handle and a flaring lip.

Height: 5¾ inches
Impressed: Hackwood
Embossed: A ribbon lozenge with **"No. 20"** impressed within and the letter **H** at the bottom right-hand corner.

* It is often very difficult to determine which of the Hackwood companies made a given jug, however, the design of this example would indicate an 1830's date, thus suggesting Wm. Hackwood.

25
Arabesque and Vines

Wm. Ridgway
c. 1835

A very rare buff coloured earthenware jug with an unusually high arching

9

handle. Arabesque motifs surround the bowl, while grape vines wander around the neck. This design appears as pattern number 4 in the first Ridgway pattern book.

Height: 6 inches
Unmarked
Courtesy of the W.J. Rees Collection

26
Daisy
William Ridgway & Co.
c. 1835

An all-over daisy pattern jug almost identical in design to the Don Pottery teapot (see Hughes no. 205f, Book 1). On the bottom, however, is the newly discovered Ridgway mark.

Height: 7¼ inches
Embossed: Newly discovered Ridgway mark with pattern no. 474 incised within.

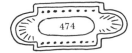

27
Camel and Elephant
Possibly Robert Bew of Bilston
c. 1840

A blue stoneware jug of modified tankard shape with a prominent foot-rim

10

and a high flaring lip. Around the bowl is a desert scene with palm trees, Indian buildings, elephants, camels and riders. This jug is unmarked, but a tan and brown stoneware example has been found bearing the mark R* BEW/ Bilston.

Height: Unknown
Unmarked
From the Morpeth Collection

28
Stylized Fuchsia and Leaves

Davenport
c. 1840

A bulbous tan stoneware jug on each side of which a cartouche made of stylized leaves encloses a hanging fuchsia flower and two daisy-like small flowers. The background is composed of a cross-stitch design and the handle is a large leaf.

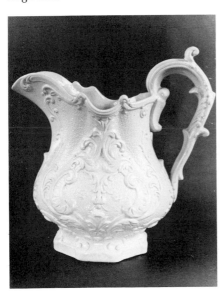

Height: 6½ inches
Impressed: Godden's Davenport mark no. 1181.

29
"Basket"

Elijah Jones
Sept. (day & year unreadable)
c. 1840

A well moulded octagonal stoneware jug with vertical hops and vines around the neck and a 3 strand basket design covering the bowl. Acanthus leaves rise on each corner and down the small foot-rim.

Height: 7 inches
Embossed:
Godden's E. Jones mark number
2213
Published by
E. Jones
Cobridge
September, (year & day unreadable)
It has been reported that this jug was registered on July 1, 1840, and a jug bearing that date has been found. The example shown in this book, however, definitely says September, although the day and year are unreadable.

30
Apple Blossom

Wm. Ridgway
c. 1840

A small cream coloured earthenware

jug with abundant enamelled leaves all around the bowl. This jug bears the Ridgway mark identified in Stoke-on-Trent only a few years ago.

Height: 4⅞ inches
Embossed: Ridgway mark with 509 in center

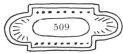

Printed in reddish brown:
3
1211
From the Cameron Hall Collection.

31
Rings and Fluting

William Ridgway & Co.
c. 1840

A beige, highly glazed stoneware jug, very bulbous in shape with a high angular handle and high flaring lip. It has been turned and thrown. The bowl is covered with many rings topped by fluting at the neck. Around the rim and lip is a wandering grapevine.

Height: 7¼ inches
Embossed: Newly found Ridgway mark with 500 impressed in the centre.

The mould for this mark was recently found by the City Museum, Stoke-on-Trent, and has impressed on the back of the mould, W. Ridgway.

From the Morpeth Collection

32
Portland Vase

Wedgwood
c. 1840

A dark blue jasper dip jug which has been thrown and sprigged. It is the Portland Vase motif depicting Pan's encounter with his beloved. (See the Alcock version of this design, Hughes number 56, Book 1). This example is done without Pan's mask. As the figures are draped, it dates past 1839. This is an interesting example as it has been turned on the inside and moulded on the outside.

Height: 8 inches
Impressed: **Wedgwood**
From the John and Linda Dohmlo Collection.

33
"Stag"
Enoch and Edward Wood
c. 1840

An example identical to the S. Hughes "Stag" jug. (See Hughes no. 41, Book 1). Many deer among foliage surround the bowl of a grey-green stoneware jug. The lip is ringed with Gothic arches, the base of the bowl with hops vines and there is a leaf handle.

Height: 9¼ inches
Impressed:
> **E. & E. Wood**
> **Burslem**

34
Acorns and Berries
Unknown
c. 1840

A low buff coloured stoneware jug with an all over design of oak leaves and acorns interspersed with grape leaves and berries. Although this is very similar to the Ridgway Acorns and Berries jug, this version has a foot-rim, and the acorn placement varies slightly.

Height: Unknown
Unmarked
From the Morpeth Collection.

35
Apprentices at Play
Unknown
c. 1840

A white stoneware jug with flow-blue underglaze trim. Each side bears the seated figures of two small boys playing. The tools around them would indicate that they have stopped work for a few minutes to play. This design is very similar to the George Ray jug. (See Hughes jug number 108, Book 1, The Dancers).

Height: 4¼ inches
Unmarked
From the Cameron Hall Collection.

John and Jennifer May in their books, ENGLISH COMMEMORATIVE POTTERY, 1780-1900 and VICTORIA REMEMBERED, illustrate many other examples of commemorative pieces including a number of jugs. This is a study unto itself.

Height: 7 inches
Unmarked
Courtesy of the W.J. Rees Collection

36
Burns and Scott

Unknown
c. 1840

A highly glazed blue earthenware jug with a bust of Sir Walter Scott on one side and Robert Burns on the other. Under the spout is a fierce mask and on the top of the handle sits a dog's head. This jug was most likely produced by a Scottish factory to honor its favorite sons.

37
"Canova"

Unknown
c. 1840

A tan stoneware jug of neo-classical design on the neck of which is a large

griffin on either side of an urn. The bowl has 12 panels containing stylized flowers and scroll work. It has a high handle, a high flaring lip and a distinct foot-rim. Canova was an Italian sculptor who lived from 1757 to 1822, and sculpted in the classical style. He was much acclaimed in his own lifetime.

Height: 9 inches
Embossed: Bust of Canova in a ring
Impressed: **J**
Impressed: **6**

38
Lady on Horseback

Unknown
c. 1840

On one side of this white stoneware jug a naked woman lies on the back of a wildly galloping horse. She is obviously in a forest as there are wild animals and much foliage. On the reverse the horse and rider have fallen to the ground among a group of eight wild horses. There is a scalloped base, a tree trunk handle and a gold band around the rim. This is obviously illustrating some work of art or fiction.

Height: 7⅞ inches
Unmarked

39
Melodrama I

Unknown
c. 1840

This jug and the one following it should be considered together. Although the shapes of the pieces dif-

fer slightly, the faces and figures are identical. It is believed that both were potted by the same company and perhaps represent all or part of a series of jugs illustrating a play or drama. On one side of this jug one finds a happy home scene with a reclining wife nursing her baby while her reclining husband looks on. A man with a gun and in a high hat stands behind her husband.

15

On the reverse the wife is running away from the man in the high hat and has her arms outstretched behind her as if to ward him off. The man holds a knife in one hand and his rifle in the other. Grey-green stoneware was used for the body of the jug.

Height: 6¼ inches
Unmarked
From the F. Bruce Leys Collection

40
Melodrama II

Unknown
c. 1840

On this jug we find the same three figures as on the above piece. Here the mother holds the baby as far away from the man in the high hat as possible. She holds her left arm up toward this man as he kneels before her. He has his hand over his heart as if he is declaring his eternal love. His knife is in his other

Height: 7½ inches
Embossed: White chrysanthemum with the number 55 in the center. This is an unidentified mark.
Impressed: **12**

41
Thistle

Unknown
c. 1840

Thistle, flowers and leaves wander all over a white stippled body.

hand. On the reverse side the man in the high hat stands with a pistol in one hand and a knife in the other over the fallen body of the husband. This jug is also made of grey-green stoneware. One has to wonder if there are more jugs to be found in this series.

Height: 7⅛ inches
Unmarked

42
King Soloman
Wood and Brownfield
September 30, 1841

A heavily decorated tan stoneware jug on which the Biblical King Soloman sits on his throne behind heavy draperies. He hands down his verdict that the child claimed by two mothers shall be split in half. Please note the similarity between this design and #'s 39 and 40, Book II.

Height: 7½ inches
Impressed:
Wood and Brownfield, Cobridge, Staffordshire Potteries September 30, 1841
From the F. Bruce Leys Collection

43
Agate
Unknown
c. 1840

A stoneware jug with a blue, black, buff

and grey agate body over which wander white ivy vines. The tree branch is very heavy in relation to the tall slender design of the bowl and neck. There is a Britannia metal lid.

Height: 10½ inches
Unmarked
From the W.J. Rees Collection

44
Hops
Jones & Walley
May 13, 1843
RD No. 7122

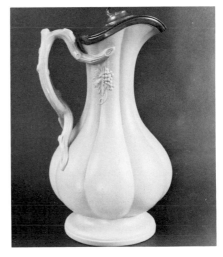

A tan stoneware jug with a plain bulbous gadrooned bowl and a very slender neck. Two crisscrossed hops vines form the handle and end at the neck in two small bunches of hops. There is a large foot-rim and a metal lid. A very graceful jug.

Height: 9½ inches
Printed in black: A double ring enclosing the words, **Registered No. 7122, 13 May 1843 by Jones & Walley, Staffs.**
Printed in center of the rings: Registration diamond

45
Arabian Nights

Samuel Alcock
c. 1845

A lavender and white parian jug with four Indians in turbans seated on a carpet amid palm trees on one side and

three Indians seated in front of a mosque on the reverse. Alcock produced three Arabian jugs: Camel, Arabian Nights and one other which is only reported. Supposedly it has tents and minerettes in its theme.

Height: 3 inches
Printed: Godden's Alcock mark number 78
Printed: **101**

46
Lace

Samuel Alcock
c. 1845

A rare lavender six-panelled jug with white lace designs in each panel and stylized acanthus leaf dividers. There is a daisy-like border around the rim and an acanthus leaf handle. The stippled ground is unusual for Alcock.

Height: 9 inches
Printed: Godden's Alcock mark number 78
Printed: **134**
From the Cameron Hall Collection

47
Love and War

Samuel Alcock
c. 1845

A white jug with lavender figures of

two mounted knights dueling beside a tree. On the reverse side the knight serenades a fair lady on horseback. The neck of the jug is surrounded by oak branches and acorns. Also seen in all blue stoneware, unmarked.

Height: 7¾ inches
Printed: Alcock Coat of Arms
Printed: **138**
From the Cameron Hall Collection

48
Mask and Acanthus
Samuel Alcock
c. 1845

A lavender jug with two large white acanthus leaves descending from the rim, a fierce satyr mask at the spout and hops vines surrounding the base. There is a tree branch handle.

Height: 6¾ inches
Printed: Godden's mark number 78
Printed: **149**
From the Cameron Hall Collection

49
Stag
Samuel Alcock
c. 1845

A design almost exactly like the S. Hughes Stag pattern. (See Hughes number 41, Book 1, and jug #33, Book 11). This, however, is a parian Alcock version with lavender stags on a white background.

Height: 8⅛ inches
Printed: Godden's Alcock mark number **78**
Printed: **119**
From the Cameron Hall Collection.

50
Mosaic
Samuel Alcock & Co.
c. 1845

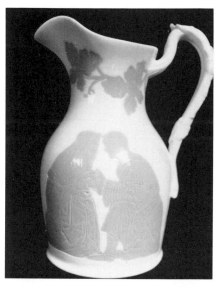

this jug is identical to Love and War, #47, Book II.

Height: 8¼ inches
Printed: Godden's Mark **78**
Printed: **144**
From the Cameron Hall Collection

51
"Punch"

Samuel Alcock & Co.
c. 1845

A white parian jug with a lavender seated Punch on one side and Punch hanging from the stage on the other. There are other assorted figures and Scrolls around the bowl. "Punch" is written on each side of the neck.

Height: 8¾ inches
Printed: Godden mark **78**
Printed: **Patent**
Printed: **154**
From the Tim Sublette Collection

A white Alcock jug in the mosaic technique with the lavender design inlaid into the ground and then incised. On one side a couple in medieval dress kneels as they exchange a ring. There is a Vestal Virgin on the reverse. It has been suggested that these represent figures from Chaucer. The shape of

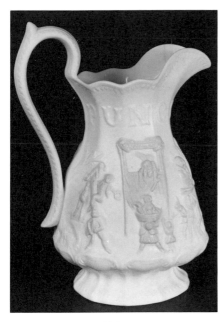

Height: 8½ inches
Unmarked
From the collection of Mrs. A.A. Love

52
Resting Shepherd

Unknown
c. 1845

A shepherd rests with his sheep on one side of this white porcelaine jug. A shepherdess stands by a stile on the reverse. The figures and foliage are crudely painted in natural colors with gilding on the wheat and rim.

53
"Chelsea Pensioners"

Unknown
c. 1845

The Chelsea Pensioners is an organization for war veterans of long service, twenty years or more, or for those who are disabled. It was founded in 1682 by Charles II at the time of the founding of the regular British Army. The members can be distinguished on the streets today by their scarlet coats and tricorn hats. This is a jug commemorating the Chelsea Pensioners and is taken from a painting believed to be by Tenniers. On one side three pensioners in their bright red coats sit around a table. On the reverse two pensioners are joined by a woman. The jug bears hops vines on the bowl and the handle is a hop vine.

Height: Unknown
Impressed in a ribbon: **Chelsea Pensioners**
Impressed in a ribbon: **Duncan Gray**
(perhaps a pensioner of that day)
From the Morpeth Collection

The design of this white stippled stoneware jug is highly reminiscent of Mason's Nesting Birds jug (Hughes number 49, Book 1). Sprays of apple blossoms are arranged in cartouches, the rim is flat and the handle is a tree branch. The shape is hexagonal and bulbous.

Height: Unknown
Unmarked
From the Morpeth Collection

55
Oak

Ridgway & Abington
December 3, 1846
RD No. 38606

The background of this entire jug is in the form of tree bark with oak leaves wandering on top. It is of stoneware, has a tree branch handle and a ceramic lid.

54
Apple Blossom

Unknown
c. 1845

Height: Unknown
Embossed: Registration diamond
Impressed:**12**
Impressed: **J**
From the Morpeth Collection

22

56
Peel and Cobden
Unknown
c. 1846

A yellow stoneware jug bearing portraits of Sir Robert Peel and Richard Cobden, the two men responsible for the repeal of the English Corn Acts in 1846. Underneath their portraits are banners bearing their names.

Height: Unknown
Unmarked
From the Morpeth Collection

57
"Sir Robert Peel"
Unknown
c. 1846

A highly glazed tan stoneware jug with a scalloped foot-rim, flat top and spout and a tree trunk handle. A large bust of Sir Robert Peel stands in deep relief on each side. There is a banner reading, "Sir Robert Peel," at the bottom and there are wandering grape vines on the bowl. Peel was instrumental in the repeal of the English Corn Acts in 1846.

Height: Unknown
Unmarked
From the Morpeth Collection

58
"Rustic"

Samuel Alcock
April 3, 1847
RD No. 42435

An all lavender jug with a bundle of twigs for lighting a fire (called faggots) surrounding the entire bowl. The bundle is tied with an ivy vine, and ivy leaves wander over the bowl.

Height: 9 1/16 inches
Printed: Diamond Registration Mark
Printed: **164**
From the Cameron Hall Collection

59
Twining Flowers

Herbert Minton & Co.
May 14, 1855
RD No. 100116

This jug is interesting because it points out the discrepancy in time between when the jug was published and when it was actually produced. On the bottom we have the diamond registration mark indicating registration on May 14, 1855. We also have the maker mark "O" for October and a symbol "X" for

1866, the actual date of production. Thus 11 years intervened. This is another graceful white parian jug with fluting at the top and bottom and a band of intertwining flowers in between. Also found in blue with white flowers.

Height: 6 inches
Impressed: Diamond Registration Mark plus maker's mark "O" for October and "X" for 1866.
From the Morpeth Collection

60
"Royal Children"

Unknown
c. 1848

A blue stoneware jug on which figures of Prince Alfred and Princess Alice, the third and fourth children of Queen Victoria, stand among garlands of hops vines. Alfred holds a bunch of hops, Alice a cluster of flowers, and both are clothed in a drape. On the feet a ribbon says, "Royal Children." These portraits were taken from sculptures by Mary Thornycroft of the four oldest children of the Queen dressed as the four seasons. Edward, Prince of Wales, represented Winter; Victoria, the Princess Royal, Summer; Alfred, Autumn; and Alice, Spring. The inspiration for the sculptures came from a play put on at Osborne by the four children in 1848.

Height: Unknown
Unmarked
From the Morpeth Collection

61
Shell and Flowers

John Rose & Co., Coalport
February 26, 1849
RD No. 58578

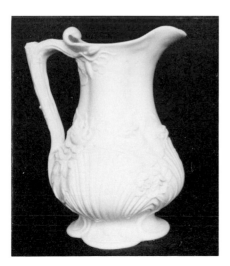

Three large shells form the bowl of this white parian jug. Flowers wander around the shells and at the top of the tree branch handle. This is a very graceful jug with a large scalloped foot.

Height: 6 inches
Impressed: Diamond Registration Mark
From the W.J. Rees Collection

61a

Jug 61 to which a lid and strainer with a large flower finial has been added. It was registered under the same registration number as above.

62
Bird and Ivy

Minton
November 17, 1849
RD Number 63718

A stippled, dark background parian jug covered with vines in which sits a blue jay type bird. On the reverse sits a very long-necked and long-legged bird. It reminds one strongly of the unmarked jug, Hughes No. 96, Book I.

Also found in parian with a vivid pink enamelled ground.

Height: 5¾ inches
Embossed: Registration diamond
Impressed: **30**
Impressed: **376**
Courtesy of the Minton Museum

elled in red. There is a branch handle enamelled in brown. This design was illustrated in the Art Journal for 1849.

Height: 7 inches
Embossed: Copeland in a cartouche
Embossed: Registration diamond
From the W.J. Rees Collection

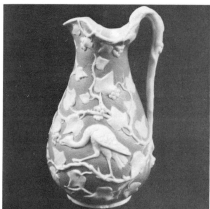

64
Diana

Edward Walley
June 21, 1850
RD No. 69884

63
Grapevine

W.T. Copeland & Sons
November 4, 1848
Reg. No. 55174

A parian jug moulded with vine leaves enamelled in green and grapes enam-

A green stoneware jug with a seated figure of Diana who has cupids and a deer at her feet. Oak leaves and acorns surround the neck of the jug.

Height: 10 inches
Applied: Registration diamond surrounded by **"Edward Walley, Villa Pottery, Cobridge, July 1850."**
From the F. Bruce Leys Collection

65
Upright Plume

W.T. Copeland & Sons
c. 1850

A white parian jug with a large luxuriant plume-like plant growing upright under basket work which surrounds the neck. There is a large foot and high handle.

Height: 8 inches
Embossed: Cartouche containing Copeland
From the W.J. Rees Collection

66
"Lily"

Samuel Alcock
c. 1850

A lavender parian ewer shaped jug with white water lilies around the bowl. This design was also illustrated by Cork

and Edge in the 1855 catalog for the Dublin Exhibition, but the Cork and Edge version was usually made of stoneware.

Height: 7½ inches
Printed: Godden's Mark **78**
Printed: **175**
From the Cameron Hall Collection

67
Shakespeare

Samuel Alcock
c. 1850

Printed: **196**
Courtesy of the City Museum, Stoke-on-Trent

68
Shepherd

Samuel Alcock & Co.
c. 1850

A lavender and white parian jug with a standing young shepherd holding a

The six lavender Shakespearean figures, The Bard, Shylock, Hamlet, Lady MacBeth, Desdemona and Julius Caesar, stand in six archways on a lovely white parian jug. There is a bearded mask at the spout, and the twin masks of comedy and tragedy are on the neck. The handle is harp-shaped and the body weight very high over a small foot-rim. Also found in all white parian and in blue painted parian with white figures. The latter bears the pattern number 223.

Height: 6 inches
Printed: Godden's Alcock Mark number **78**

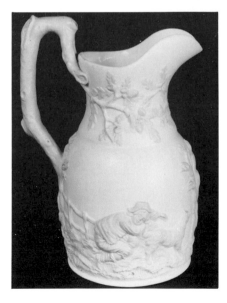

baby lamb and accompanied by his dog and other sheep. On the other side the shepherd kneels beside a fence holding the lamb while his dog keeps watch. The neck is surrounded by an oak leaf branch with acorns which continues on to form the handle.

Height: 7¾ inches
Printed: Godden's mark **78**
Printed: **Patent**
Printed: **Samuel Alcock & Co.**

69
Grapes and Bows

Bradbury, Anderson and Bettanny
c. 1850

On a light lavender stippled body are white panels and grape vines. In the middle of each panel is a bow from which hangs a swag of grapevines and grapes. There is a grapevine handle.

Height: 6½ inches
Printed: The Royal Arms of Alcock with "Patent" underneath. See Godden's mark #78. The signature however is BA&B instead of Alcock.

70
Vintage

Bradbury, Anderson and Bettanny
c. 1850

The design on one side of this jug is almost identical to that on Hughes jug number 126, shown on page 83 of *A Collectors Guide to Nineteenth Century Jugs, Book 1*. The shape, however, is more bulbous on this example, with a higher body weight and much less defined foot-rim. The colour of the body is a light lavender. Both the mark on the bottom of the jug and the lavender colour make this jug very easy to mistake for an Alcock piece, but the impressed initials B.A. and B. indicate production by Bradbury, Anderson and Bettanny. Also found in high quality white parian.

Height: 5¼ inches
Printed: Coat of Arms (in black)
Printed: **BA & B**

71
Hunt

W.T. Copeland and Sons
c. 1850-1867

A hunt scene with white applied figures on a pink stoneware body typical of the 1820's, however, the impressed Copeland mark would date this jug circa 1850 to 1867.

Height: 5⅛ inches
Impressed: **Copeland**

73
"Old and New Flower"
James Dudson
c. 1850

Large upright sprays of stylized oriental poppies surround the bowl of a light green stippled stoneware jug. Above two raised bands at the neck, hops vines grow freely. There is a small foot-rim and slightly flaring lip and handle.

Height: 8 inches
Impressed: Dudson

72
Egg and Dart
W.T. Copeland & Sons
c. 1850

A very graceful white parian jug with high lip and handle, narrow neck and fairly pronounced foot-rim which has been decorated with the egg and dart border design. Stylized pendant flowers surround the neck and stylized leaves the bowl. It gives much the effect of a Greek Urn.

Height: 6¾ inches
Impressed: **Copeland**

74
Helmeted Lady
Gille Factory, France
c. 1850

A white bisque jug with a helmeted female face which extends from under the lip to the foot-rim. At the top of the lady's helmet is a fierce mask which is repeated at the base of the handle. Various borders surround the foot-rim and the neck. The shape of this jug is most unusual in that it has an extremely high handle and a very small opening at the rim. The Gille pottery was founded in France in 1845 and hired Charles Baury to do their modeling. This helmeted female face could be Joan of Arc.

Height: 6¼ inches
Embossed: Blue lozenge containing the intertwined letters **G** and **J**.

75
Stylized Grapes and Scrolls
Possibly Minton
c. 1850

A very unusual shaped blue and white parian jug. There is a tiny foot-rim with a very low bulbous disk-like bowl, a narrow neck and a sensuous handle. Stylized flowers and scrolls surround the top of the bowl.

Height: 4½ inches
Incised: **480**
Christie's S. Kensington sold a similar jug and attributed it to Minton in their catalogue. The incised 480 and the quality of the piece would seem to bear this out.
From the W.J. Rees Collection

76
"Cascades"

United States Pottery Co.
Bennington, Vermont
c. 1850

This parian jug of unusual design is one of the few moulded jug patterns designed by the Bennington Company rather than copied from British prototypes. It is said to have been inspired by Niagra Falls.

Height: 8¾ inches
Embossed:
United States Pottery Co.
Bennington, Vt.
From the Cameron Hall Collection

mark number **3988**
From the W.J. Rees Collection

77
Cain and Abel

Edward Walley
c. 1850

Another tan stoneware Cain and Abel motif, this time potted by Edward Walley. (Compare Hughes jug number 89, Book 1, the Alcock example of this design).

Height: 10 inches
Printed: Coat of Arms
Printed in black: **Edward Walley,**
Cobridge, Staffordshire. Godden's

78
Arrowhead Leaves

Unknown
c. 1850

Stylized arrowhead upright leaves alternate with equally stylized upright flowers on the bowl and around the neck of a grey-blue stoneware jug. This piece has been well glazed inside and out.

Height: Unknown
Unmarked
From the Morpeth Collection

Height: 8½ inches

Unmarked

79
Classical
Unknown
c. 1850

Nine classical figures of musicians, dancers, etc. surround the green stoneware body. There is engine turning at the base and hops vines around the neck ending in a hops vine handle.

80
The Bathers
Unknown
c. 1850

White bisque jug portraying two nude female figures bathing among the rushes. A vine encircles the neck. It is interesting because the handle, rim, inside and bottom fourth of the bowl are heavily glazed, while the rest of the surface is totally unglazed. Around the inside of the rim is a band of gilded

leaves and berries.

Height: 3½ inches
Unmarked

Unmarked
From the Morpeth Collection

81
Good Samaritan
Unknown
c. 1850

On each side of a large white stoneware jug is a good Samaritan scene. The wealthy nobleman kneels beside the fallen traveller to give him aid and comfort. In the background is a kneeling camel and much foliage.

Height: 9¾ inches
Unmarked

83
Iris

Unknown
c. 1850

A beautifully executed large iris design in white sits on a blue ground in very deep relief. There is a tree branch handle and scalloped rim.

82
Grapevine and Barley
Unknown
c. 1850

A white stoneware jug with undecorated bowl, high flaring lip and handle and medium sized foot-rim. The neck bears a grape vine and the lip has sprays of barley.

Height: Unknown

Height: 8½ inches
Unmarked
From the Mrs. A.A. Love Collection

84
"Now I'm Grandpapa"

Unknown
c. 1850

A charming sentimental Victorian jug of white parian. In a cartouche on one side a little girl sits in her grandfather's chair wearing his glasses, smoking his pipe and reading his paper. At the bottom of the cartouche is incised, "NOW I'M GRANDPAPA." On the reverse side of the jug the little girl sits in her grandmother's chair holding Grandma's knitting and wearing her glasses. A playful kitten plays with a ball of yarn. Under this cartouche is incised, "NOW I'M GRANDMAMA." Scrolls and vertical blue stippled bands surround the cartouches.

85
Hazelnut

Unknown
c. 1850

A stoneware jug with vertical stalks of wheat and leaves rising from a small foot-rim. Around the neck is a spray of hazelnut.

Height: 8½ inches
Unmarked
From the Timothy Sublette Collection

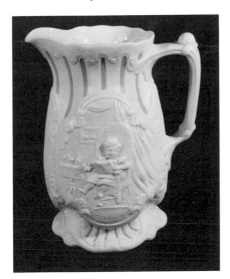

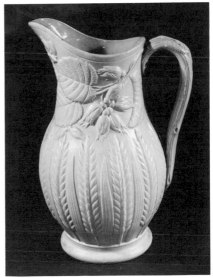

Height: Unknown
Unmarked
From the Morpeth Collection

86
Hops

Unknown
c. 1850

Sprays of hops and hops berries surround the bowl of a white parian jug. There is a scalloped rim and a kidney shaped ring inside the tree branch handle.

Height: 11 inches
Unmarked
From the W.J. Rees Collection

88
Iris

Unknown
c. 1850

A blue stoneware jug covered with large white irises and leaves. There is an iris bud on the handle.

Height: 8 inches
Unmarked

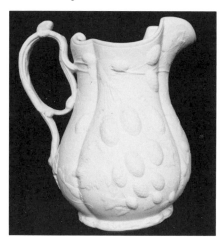

87
Landscape

Unknown
c. 1850

A dark blue parian ewer with white moulded flowers framing a painted country landscape. Upright acanthus leaves surround the base.

Height: 9 inches
Unmarked
From the W.J. Rees Collection

89
Renaissance

Unknown
c. 1850

A white stippled stoneware jug with a small flat foot-rim. There is gadrooning around the bottom of the bowl and guilloche bands around the top of the bowl and the neck. A lappet border surrounds the flat rim.

Height: Unknown
Unmarked
From the Morpeth Collection

flowers and leaves on a highly glazed stoneware jug. At the top of the high flaring handle is a small leaf almost standing straight up. The base has smaller upright flowers separated by banding.

Height: Unknown
Unmarked
From the Morpeth Collection

90
Rose

Unknown
c. 1850

A large rose is surrounded by many

91
"Ceres"

Edward Walley
April 26, 1851
RD No. 78634

A grey-green stoneware jug with metal lid and an irregular shape. Instead of a foot-rim, the jug seems to rest on a band of foliage and flowers from which rise stalks of barley. The handle is a tree branch which continues on to the bowl of the jug ending in tree leaves.

Height: 7½ inches
Printed: Godden's E. Walley mark number **3988**
Embossed: Registration diamond with **"Ceres"** at the bottom
Impressed: **21**

92
"Rossi"
T.J. & J. Mayer
Registered Jan. 21, 1845
c. 1851 Produced
Reg. No. 25199

There is a question as to whether this 1851 jug should be allowed to be called "Rossi," as Mayer considerably modified the design compared to the line drawing which they submitted to the Design Registration office in 1845. (Compare the two pictures below.) The overall effect is the same, but the porportions, design of the handle and the borders are different. Both examples contain five Bacchus heads, wandering grape vines and arrangements of acanthus leaves. When the "Rossi" jug was presented to the Art-Union in 1845, the journal printed a review of the jug in part as follows: ". . . It is liable to some objections: the neck is too ponderous for the base; the handle is somewhat too thin and short; and the body, in front, presents an angle which takes from its grace of form." Obviously when Mayer presented the second version of the jug to the public at the Exhibition in 1851, they tried to correct some of these criticisms. The pattern for both jugs was a modification of designs from Rossi's famous collection of antique vases. The body is white parian. Drawing from the Design Registration Books in the Public Records Office — #25199

Height: 7¾ inches
Printed in sepia: **Godden's TJ & J Mayer mark no. 2571**
Printed in sepia: **Prize Medal 1851**

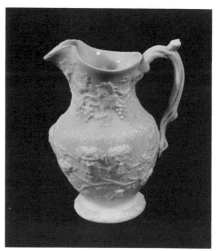

93
Mermaid, Merman and Cupid

Minton and Co.
Sept. 16, 1852
RD #86657

A beautifully designed and executed

white parian jug with large figures of a mermaid and a merman holding hands with Cupid who is standing on a large shell. Ivy leaves wander on the background. There is a mask of Neptune at the base. On the bottom half of the bowl are fourteen panels, with an Elizabethan strapwork panel alternating with an empty panel. The egg and dart border encircles the foot-rim. The registration diamond on the bottom of this jug indicates a date of May 18, 1852, but the picture from the registration office gives a date of September 16, 1852.

Height: 10¾ inches
Embossed: Registration diamond
From the F. Bruce Leys Collection

94
Greek Key

Minton
Registered: June 5, 1852
Year cypher: 1843
RD No. 85248

This celadon and white parian jug is covered with two bands of fluting sepa-

rated by an applied Greek key design at the neck. It was thrown on a wheel. There can be no mistaking the marks on the bottom of the jug as they are very clear and distinct. This makes it difficult to understand why the cypher mark indicating a manufacture date of 1843 is nine years in advance of the registration date of 1852.

Height: 5 inches
Embossed: Registration diamond
Impressed: year cypher   △
Courtesy of the V. & A. Museum, London

95
Medieval Revelry

Minton
July 23, 1852
Registration #85803-4

A beautiful quality white Minton parian jug with hand-moulded and applied figures in deep relief. On the front a medieval couple are dancing, a man under the spout is smoking and two men on the reverse are drinking. The piece would seem to portray the various entertainment of medieval life.

Height: 9 inches
Applied and Impressed: Registration diamond
From the Mrs. A.A. Love Collection

96
Ivy

Minton
September 3, 1852
RD No. 86473

A celadon green parian jug with white mouldings of wandering ivy. There is a high flaring handle and a deeply scalloped neck rim.

Height: 5 inches
Impressed: Diamond registration mark
Impressed: **475**
From the W.J. Rees Collection and the Timothy Sublett Collection

97
"The Alhambra"

Ridgway, Son & Co.
c. 1852

A six panelled tan stoneware jug covered with Moorish motifs. Though rare, there are two examples of this jug in the W.J. Rees Collection, this one and a 4 inch parian one. The design appeared in the Art Journal for May

1852, as a late Ridgway and Abington product, however, this jug bears the earlier Ridgway, Son and Co. mark.

Height: 8 inches
Impressed: **Ridgway, Son and Co.**
From the W.J. Rees Collection

98
Harvest Barrel

W.T. Copeland & Sons
February 26, 1853
RD No. 89958

A white stoneware jug with a stays and barrel shape. On each side is a large spray of wheat, oats and barley. It is flat topped and has an angular handle.

Height: 9 inches
Embossed: A shield bearing an impressed Copeland and the number **9**
Embossed: Registration diamond

99
"Lily"

Livesley, Powell & Co.
June 14, 1853
Registration #91405

A stoneware jug with white calla lillies and green and yellow foliage against a bright pink ground.

Height: 8½ inches
Impressed and Embossed: Registration Diamond with **"Lily"** above and **"Livesley, Powell & Co."** below.
From the Cameron Hall Collection

100
David and Goliath

Thomas Till & Son
June 3, 1854
Registration #96003

41

A Thomas Till religious theme. This time it portrays David killing the fallen Goliath on one side with David being embraced by the lovely Bathsheba on the reverse. The body is of white stippled stoneware enamelled emerald green.

Height: 9 inches
Applied: Diamond Registration Mark
Impressed: **Till & Son**
From the Cameron Hall Collection

101
"Royal Patriotic Jug"
Samuel Alcock & Co.
January 1, 1855

During the Crimean War a Royal Commission set up a Patriotic Fund to raise money for the support of families left behind by war casualties of the army, navy and marines. The President of the Commission was Prince Albert. On January 1, 1855 Samuel Alcock published this Royal Patriotic Jug and sold it to help raise money for the fund. The jug is made of white glazed porcelain with a sentimental transfer print on each side. One side features a group of wounded and dying soldiers on the battlefield; the other a weeping mother and sorrowful child. Flying overhead is an angel bearing a banner which reads, "Royal Patriotic Fund." There is a dog's head handle and the jug is decorated with red and gold. The scene on the bowl is not marked.

Height: 7½ inches
Printed: A lovely, ornate grouping of crown, banners, cannon, bayonet, etc. in the center of which are the words:
The Royal Patriotic Jug
Published
by
S. Alcock & Co.
Hill Pottery
Burslem
Jan. 1, 1855
A registration diamond is incorporated.

102
Babes in the Wood
Cork and Edge
c. 1855

A marked example of Hughes jug number 129, Book 1. This Cork and Edge American Eagle mark was also used on the Cup Tosser jug #125, Book I.

Height: 6½ inches

Printed: Godden's Cork and Edge mark no. **1099**

Embossed: Ribbon bearing the impressed words **"Botanic"** and **"Cork and Edge"**

103
"Botanic"
Cork and Edge
c. 1855

A blue stippled stoneware jug with a white vine twining all around the bowl. There is a white rim at the top and on the foot. The jug has a tree branch handle.

Height: 8 inches

104
"Peace and Plenty"
Probably Cork & Edge
c. 1855

A creamy white stippled stoneware jug with straight sides and a high body weight. On each side a classical lady in a position of movement carries a horn of plenty in one hand and an olive branch in the other. The caption reads, "Peace and Plenty." A marked example has been reported.

Height: 7¾ inches
Unmarked

105
"May They Ever be United"
James Dudson
c. 1855

A tan stoneware Crimean War jug with the Arms of England applied in very deep relief on one side. Above this are the Coats of Arms of Turkey and

France. A banner reads, "May We Ever be United." All of the above is set in a sea of painted leaves. On the reverse side are represented the Arms of Austria and Russia. Stippling was used on the plain surfaces.

Height: 8½ inches
Impressed: **Dudson**
Impressed: B

A beautiful quality white parian jug decorated with six arcades containing trailing ivy branches. Acanthus leaves decorate the handle. This is a piece from the Kerr and Binns period of Worcester.

Height: 9 inches
Printed: A rare Worcester mark, Godden's mark number **4348**

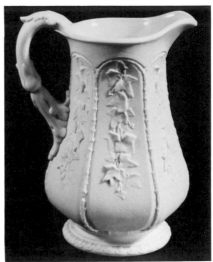

107
"Ino"

Samuel Alcock
c. 1855

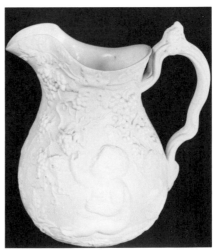

106
Trailing Ivy

W.H. Kerr & Co.
c. 1860

A lavender parian "Ino" pattern jug like the Cork and Edge version. (See Hughes #128, Book 1).

Height: 5¾ inches
Printed: Godden Mark **78**
Printed: **Samuel Alcock & Co.**
Printed: **193**
From the Timothy Sublette Collection

108
"Honeysuckle"
Charles Meigh and Son
c. 1855

A blue and white stoneware jug with an interesting "loop-de-loop" handle. There is a bulbous bowl with low body weight and a very long gadrooned neck, which is topped with a horizontal band of stylized flowers and leaves. Six circles surround the bowl containing a single honeysuckle blossom. Leaves and vines tie the circles together. This is a very dramatic, unusual design.

Height: 8 inches
Applied: Roundel containing **C. Meigh and Son, Hanley**
From the W.J. Rees Collection

109
The Prodigal Son
Till and Son
c. 1855

A grey-green stoneware tankard jug incorporating the figures of the Biblical Prodigal Son embracing his father. The figures of this jug are surrounded by tropical foliage, the rim is scalloped and almost flat and the handle is of bamboo design. A bamboo design encircles the rim and foot.

Height: 6½ inches
Impressed: **Till & Son**

110
The Muses
Thomas Till & Son
c. 1855

A white stippled stoneware tankard which has two muses, one on each side. One holds a lyre and the other holds a horn of plenty. At their head is a cherub in flight. There is tropical foliage at the front and back seams and a foliage handle.

Height: 7¼ inches
Impressed: **Till & Son**

Hughes number 128, Book 1, and number 107, Book II.)

Height: 9 inches
Printed in black: Coat of Arms over Edward Walley, Cobridge, Staffordshire. Godden's mark number **3988**
Impressed: **E. Walley, Cobridge**
From the W.J. Rees Collection

112
Oriental Poppy
Samuel Alcock
c. 1855

A blue parian jug with white oriental poppies around the bowl. An unusual design for Alcock.

Height: 8 inches
Printed: Godden's mark **78**
Printed: **261**
From the Timothy Sublette Collection

111
"Ino"
Edward Walley, Cobridge
c. 1855

A white stoneware jug apparently identical to the "Ino" design illustrated by Cork and Edge in the Paris Exhibition of 1855. This one, however, bears the mark of Edward Walley. (Compare to

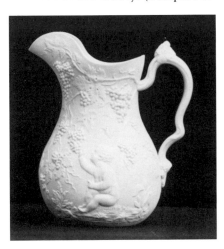

113
Jug of All Nations
Unknown
Designer: Either George Baguley or Henry Baggaley
c. 1855

This jug commemorated the nineteen nations which took part in the 1855 Paris Exhibition. It is a very ornate white stoneware jug in three tiers, totally covered with the insignia of the nineteen nations separated by strap work. Each insignia is headed by the name of the country represented. Great Britain is on the spout. The countries which took part in the exhibition are as follows: Denmark, Switzerland, Turkey, Portugal, Brazil, Sweden, Greece, Bavaria, Austria, Russia, France, Belgium, Holland, America and Sardinia.

Height: 14½ inches
Unmarked: A jug of this pattern was sold by Sotheby's and attributed to (sic) "Baggley"

114
Hops and Barley
Minton & Co.
February 9, 1857
RD #108930

A white parian jug gadrooned around the bottom, with hops wandering around the waist. A band of arcades surround the neck, each with a sheaf of barley.

Height: 5 inches
Impressed: Diamond registration mark
Impressed: Minton year mark for 1857
Impressed: **530**
From the W.J. Rees Collection

115
"Oporto"
E & W Walley
May 7, 1859
Registration #115953

47

Hops vines and berries ending in a hops vine handle surround the body and neck of this white stoneware jug. The background is most interesting as it is composed of thousands of tiny raised circles each containing an incised dot. The effect is of stippling.

Height: 10 inches
Embossed: Registration Diamond with the name **"Oporto"** underneath.

116
Tulip and Sunflower
Probably Cork and Edge
c. 1857

A white parian jug with large tulips and sunflowers on the bowl. The bowl, base and rim have a scalloped contour. It was illustrated by Cork and Edge in the catalogue of the British Section at the Paris Universal Exhibition of 1855, and Barrett illustrates a Bennington marked example and a C.W. Clark Co. marked example in his book on Bennington.

Height: 8¼ inches
Unmarked
From the Cameron Hall Collection

117
Roses
Minton
c. 1858

A white parian jug with roses freely growing over the bowl. There is a scalloped flat rim.

Height: 2½ inches
Impressed: **261**
Impressed: **54**
From the Minton Museum, Stoke-on-Trent

118
Moses and the Rock
Ridgway and Abington
January 1, 1859
(the 1 is indistinct)

48

A grey green stoneware tankard jug with an E shaped handle, a flat rim and a slightly flaring lip. On each side of the bowl a figure of Moses stands beside a stream on the Mount as he strikes the rock of Horeb. See the Bible, Exodus 17:3-6. There is a border of stylized leaves at the top and the bottom.

Height: 5½ inches
Embossed:　**Godden's**
Ridgway mark number 3249
Published by
E. Ridgway & Abington
Hanley
January 1, 1859 ?

119
Shamrock
William Brownfield
May 20, 1859
RD No. 119968

A diaper design of hundreds of shamrocks stand row on row under round arches on a stippled background of this white stoneware jug. There is a raised handle.

Height: Unknown
Embossed: Godden's Brownfield mark number 661 with impressed 12

Embossed: Diamond registration mark
Impressed: **M**
From the Morpeth Collection

120
"Victoria Regina"
Sanford Pottery
July 6, 1860
RD No. 130462

A very rare white stoneware Sanford Commemorative jug of very similar design to the jug, Hughes number 141, Book I, "The Loyal Volunteers." There is an all over design of beaded strapwork, borders, leaves and berries. A portrait of young Victoria is in an olive cartouche flanked by the initial "V" on one side and "R" on the reverse. This jug is believed to have been designed for Victoria's silver jubilee which never took place because of the death of Prince Albert on Dec. 14, 1861.

Height: 9¾ inches
Embossed: Registration diamond

Dudson fern and snowdrop sprigging (called by the company "Acanthus and Bluebell"). There is a white oak leaf collar at the elongated neck, a scalloped lip and a tree branch handle. Also found in a 2 handled sugar bowl with lid. See 121a, Book II.

Height: 9 inches
Incised: **391** with the nine and one very elongated.

Impressed: 2 ribbons bearing the words **"Sanford"** and **"Pottery"**

121
"Acanthus and Bluebell"
James Dudson
c. 1860

A cobalt blue jasper jug with white

121a
"Acanthus and Bluebell"
sugar bowl

122 "Apple Blossom"
James Dudson
c. 1860

A white stippled stoneware jug with freely growing apple blossoms covering the bowl. There is fluting around the neck, and the piece stands on a small foot-rim. The tree branch handle is interesting as it does not start at the rim, but at the top of the stippling, making it quite short for the height of the jug.

Height: Unknown
Unmarked
Identified by Mrs. Derek Dudson
Courtesy of the Derek Dudson Family

123
Hawthorn

R.S. Hill
c. 1860

An interestingly shaped white stippled jug with lavender flowering branches surrounding the bowl. These are quite possibly hawthorn blossoms, which

grow out of a lavender twig handle. The neck is fluted. R.S. Hill would seem to be one of the firms who occupied the Hill Pottery, Burselem after Samuel Alcock left. They continued to

use the Alcock Coat of Arms and pattern numbering system.

Height: 7½ inches
Black Printed: Coat of Arms
Black Printed: Patent No. **278**
Black Printed: **R.S.H.**
From the W.J. Rees Collection

124
Crocus

James Dudson
c. 1860

A light blue stoneware jug with a large spray of crocus on each side. The crocuses are trimmed in yellow and orange, and cobalt blue has been used around the rim, down the front and for flower stems and leaves. The jug gives a flow blue effect.

Height: 8 inches
Printed in red: **171**
This jug was identified by Mrs. Derek Dudson

125
"Fuchsia"

James Dudson
c. 1860

A blue stippled stoneware jug with fuchsia flowers and leaves cascading all around the bowl.

Height: 7¼ inches
Impressed: **Dudson**

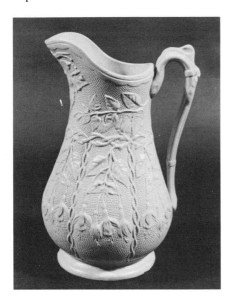

127
Poppy
James Dudson
c. 1860

A highly glazed white stoneware jug with large dark blue poppies on the bowl. The rim is edged in dark blue.

Height: Unknown
Authenticated by Mrs. Derek Dudson
Courtesy of the Derek Dudson Family

126
"Night and Morning"
James Dudson
c. 1860

A light blue stoneware jug with a large cartouche on each side. Inside one cartouche an angel in flight carries two sleeping children followed by a little bird in flight. The reverse side shows the angel dropping flower petals with a wide awake child on her back. These scenes represent morning and night and are modeled from two bas-reliefs by Bertel Thorwaldsen. The neck and base of the jug bear branches of leaves and berries. Also found in grey-green stoneware.

Height: 8 inches
Unmarked
Identified by Mrs. Derek Dudson

128
"Spring and Summer"
James Dudson
c. 1860

A white stoneware jug with a group of three Cupids playing instruments on one side of the bowl, while the three cupids hold a long ribbon on the reverse. There is Elizabethan strapwork at the neck and alternating stylized flowers and acanthus leaves on the base.

Height: Unknown
Unmarked
Identified by Mrs. Derek Dudson
Courtesy of the Derek Dudson Family

129
"Sunflower"
James Dudson
c. 1860

A blue stoneware jug with very large flowers and leaves on an unusual background. Instead of stippling, tiny circles were used for the background.

Height: Unknown
Unmarked
This jug was authenticated by Mrs. Derek Dudson
From the Morpeth Collection

130
"Tulip"
James Dudson
c. 1860

A white stoneware jug on which large tulips, buds and leaves fill the bowl. There is an unusual type of stippling

53

composed of hundreds of tiny bubbles of clay.

Height: Unknown
Unmarked
Authenticated by Mrs. Derek Dudson
Courtesy of the Derek Dudson Family

131
Vertical Leaves

James Dudson
c. 1860

Small vertical leaves on an upright stem are separated by equally long pointed leaves all around the bowl of a grey-green stoneware jug. There is a guilloche border around the neck.

Height: 7½ inches
Impressed: **Dudson**

132
"Vine Border"

James Dudson
c. 1860

A white stippled stoneware jug with gadrooning at the bottom and a hops trellis pattern around the bowl. There is a little rosette on the handle. This jug was undecorated in the 1860's, but in the 1870's, enamelling was added.

Height: 7½ inches
Unmarked
Identified by Mrs. Derek Dudson
From the Morpeth Collection

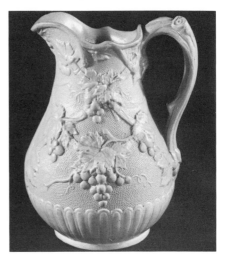

132a
An enamelled version of "Vine Border" c. 1870

133
Shells

Unknown
c. 1860

A taupe colored stoneware jug with a large scalloped foot rim, high spout and tree branch handle. The rim and foot-rim are edged in dark blue. Applied dark taupe water lilies wander around the bowl above four large moulded shells.

Height: 9½ inches
Unmarked

135
Upright Ivy

Morley and Ashworth
c. 1860

A buff coloured stoneware jug with ten panels each containing upright stalks of ivy. There is a tree branch handle.

Height: 6½ inches
Impressed: **Morley and Ashworth, Hanley**
From the W.J. Rees Collection

134
Ivy Leaves

Kerr & Binns Worcester
c. 1860

A beautifully moulded white parian jug with a twisted handle, ivy leaves surrounding the neck and two rows of gadrooning around the bowl.

Height: 6¼ inches
Printed in Blue: Godden's Worcester mark number **4345**

136
Acanthus

Unknown
c. 1860

A white stoneware jug with stippled background on which stylized acanthus leaves are surrounded by beaded strapwork.

Height: Unknown
Unmarked
From the Morpeth Collection

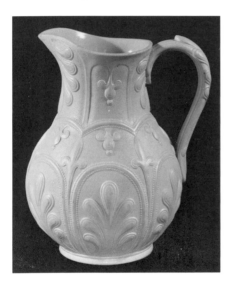

138
Apple Blossoms

Unknown
c. 1860

Naturalistic wandering apple blossom branches surround the bowl of a white stippled stoneware jug. The design is enamelled in naturalistic colors.

Height: 6½ inches
Impressed: :˙:
From the Cameron Hall Collection

137
Acanthus

Unknown
c. 1860

A white stoneware jug with six large acanthus leaves rising from a band around the bowl. At the neck is a grape-like leaf falling from the spout. Around the bottom of the jug are more grape leaves and some stylized flowers.

Height: Unknown
Unmarked
From the Morpeth Collection

139
Aquatic

Probably Wilkinson & Rickhuss
Registered June 19, 1857
Reg. #110161

This jug is most likely English, however, it was also made in Bennington, Vermont and is illustrated in Mr. Barrett's book. He calls it "Lily Pad," however, the leaf is very questionably that of a lily. The jug is made of white parian and has large aquatic leaves surrounding the bowl.

Height: 7¼ inches
Impressed: Unreadable Registration Diamond
From the Cameron Hall Collection

141
Birds and Bamboo

Unknown
c. 1860

Bamboo stalks curve around the bowl of a flat-sided stoneware jug. Three birds sit and fly among the stalks on one side, two birds on the reverse. A bamboo stalk goes around the generous foot-rim, down the handle and around the rim and spout.

Height: Unknown
Unmarked
From the Morpeth Collection

140
Barley Stalk

Unknown
c. 1860

A white stippled stoneware jug with upright stalks of barley standing in strapwork.

Height: Unknown
Unmarked
From the Morpeth Collection

142
Blackberry

Unknown
c. 1860

A blue stoneware jug with horizontal branches of blackberries growing around the bowl. Side by side leaf tops make a border on the base, above which runs a vitruvian scroll.

Height: 6½ inches
Unmarked

144
Cartouche

Unknown
c. 1860

This white bisque pitcher has an empty scroll-like cartouche on each side. The interesting feature is the very high spout.

Height: 4 inches
Unmarked
From the Cameron Hall Collection

143
The Bull

Unknown
c. 1860

A highly glazed earthenware white jug with cobalt blue and copper lustre decoration. There is a lotus border around the rim. A big bull looks over a fence obviously scaring the assembled crowd. Ladies throw their arms around their male protectors.

Height: 8 inches
Unmarked
From the F. Bruce Leys Collection

145
Cupid and Psyche

Unknown
c. 1860

A fine quality white parian jug portraying Cupid and Psyche on a wall surrounded by trees and foliage. This design is illustrated as made by Bennington in Richard Carter Barrett's book on that company. It is also listed as number 22 in Alcock's display for the 1851 Great Exhibition. This example could be by either company.

Height: 8 inches
Unmarked
From the F. Bruce Leys Collection

146
Drama

Unknown
c. 1860

A white parian jug moulded in ribs with brightly coloured moulded figures depicting characters from a play. (Compare to Hughes jug number 154, Book 1, Shakespeare). The W.J. Rees collection has three of these small parian jugs with theatrical themes which are probably taken from Shakespearean plays.

Height: 4½ inches
Unmarked
From the W.J. Rees Collection

147
Flower Stalks
Unknown
c. 1860

A white stoneware jug covered with upright growing flowers on a stippled background. The moulding is very sharp.

Height: 6 inches
Unmarked

148
Foxglove
Unknown
c. 1860

A stippled stoneware jug with blue background and large white foxglove flowers and leaves all around. There is a metal lid.

Height: 8¼ inches
Unmarked
From the Cameron Hall Collection

149
Grapevine and Barrel
Unknown
c. 1860

The entire bowl of the white stoneware jug is in the shape of a barrel and stays

which are covered with wandering grapevines. The handle is in the shape of a backward capital E.

Height: 8½ inches
Unmarked

150
Hops
Unknown
c. 1860

White hops vines surround a white earthenware jug with orange background. A ribbon swag intertwines with the vines and culminates at the peak of the swag with a bow tie. The jug is highly glazed.

Height: 7 inches
Unmarked
From the Cameron Hall Collection

151
Hops

Unknown
c. 1860

A white stoneware jug with all over design of hops, acanthus leaves and scrolls. It was reproduced in the 1920's by Portmerien Pottery and is being reproduced again today. See jug number 231, Book II.

Height: Unknown
Unmarked
From the Morpeth Collection

152
Hunt Jug

Unknown
c. 1860

A grey-green stoneware jug with two hunters, two dogs and dead game on each side. There is a metal lid.

Height: 6 inches
Unmarked

153
Lily

Unknown
c. 1860

A large branch of white lillies rise from a cluster of long white spiked leaves on the dark green ground of this stoneware jug. There is gilt on the handle, lip and foot-rim.

Height: 7¾ inches
Unmarked

154
Mandarin

Unknown
c. 1860

A white bisque jug whose entire bowl is in the shape of a kneeling Oriental man with a long sinister moustache. Multicoloured enamels have been used to decorate the figure. A small oriental head stands on top of the handle.

Height: 4½ inches
Impressed: 18
Impressed: ✕
From the Cameron Hall Collection

155
Mistletoe

Unknown
c. 1860

A small blue stoneware jug with mistletoe branches wandering around the bowl.

Height: 3⅝ inches
Unmarked
From the Cameron Hall Collection

156
Pendant

Unknown
c. 1860

Intertwined renaissance strapwork, ending at the top and bottom in a pendant, covers the bowl of a white stipple stoneware body. The diamond strapwork forms the handle.

Height: Unknown
Unmarked
From the Morpeth Collection

157
Poppy and Acanthus

Unknown
c. 1860

A grey-green jug with a large poppy and bud on each side. These are set among upright acanthus leaves. The design is highly reminiscent of Dudson.

Height: 6¼ inches
Unmarked
From the Cameron Hall Collection

flanked by morning glories is on each side of the bowl under which stands fence-like banding. At the neck and the foot is a band of upright leaf tops. The neck of the jug is covered with a trellis design forming diamonds with a rosette in each diamond.

Height: Unknown
Unmarked
From the Morpeth Collection

159
Rose and Thistle

Unknown
c. 1860

158
Rose and Convolvulus

Unknown
c. 1860

A white stippled stoneware jug with a flaring lip and low handle. A large rose

An arrangement of white roses and thistles on a dark stippled ground is placed in six cartouches on a white stoneware jug. The rim is outlined in dark green. Perhaps the theme has to do with the Rose of England and the Thistle of Scotland.

Height: 7 inches
Painted in dark green: **8**

161
Twining Flowers
Unknown
c. 1860

A blue stoneware jug with large flowers and leaves freely growing on the bowl.

Height: 5 inches
Unmarked

160
Sea Shell
Unknown
c. 1860
A tiny white stoneware jug in the shape of a large sea shell. There is a tree branch handle.

Height: 3¾ inches
Unmarked
From the Cameron Hall Collection

162
"Barley"*
James Dudson
April 25, 1861
RD No. 140200

A grey-green stoneware jug with stalks of wheat and wheat leaves covering the bowl. It was produced in two forms: one with wheat stalks at the neck pointing toward the handle and a distinct foot-rim, the other with acanthus leaves at the spout, a smaller foot-rim, and the spray of wheat at the neck pointing toward the spout.

Height: 8 inches
Unmarked: Identified from design books in the Public Record Office, Kew, England.

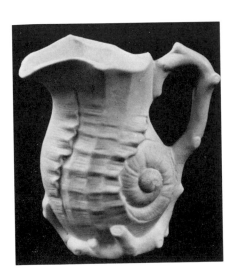

*This jug was called "Barley" by Dudson, although the grain is definitely wheat. Dudson produced two versions of this pattern.

163

The second "Barley" design by Dudson with the wheat pointing toward the spout.

164
"Doric"

Josiah Wedgwood
Registered Nov. 29, 1861
Potted March 1865
RD No. 146924

Wedgwood experimented several times with an agate appearing body. In his early experiments the agate design went all through the body. Later it was only on the surface. This little brown jug is of the later type. It has been thrown then decorated with a moulded mask at the spout and bands of gilt at the rim, neck and base.

Height: 5½ inches
Impressed: **Doric**
Impressed: **Wedgwood**
Impressed: **HRS** (date of potting)
Impressed: **30**

165
Gothic Floral

Beech & Hancock
July 14, 1862
RD No. 153127

Six white stalks of stylized flowers on long stems are set in six white cartouches outlined in gold. There is gold trim at the neck, handle and foot on a bright green stippled ground. A lappet border surrounds the lip. This jug was also produced in lavender.

Height: 9 inches
Printed: Registration diamond
Printed in black: Beech and Hancock
Swan Bank
Tunstall
Painted in green: **258**

166
Cashmore "Everybody's Clown"
Elsmore and Forster
1863

A white glazed earthenware jug with a full length transfer print portrait of Joe Cashmore, the clown, on each side. Under the spout the "Set to," "Knock down blow" and "Death" scenes from a cock fight are presented. In the middle of the transfer prints of the cock fight are painted the initials of the owner of the jug, W.S.D. and the date 1863. This is a puzzle jug with a secret place for liquid and holes with which to control it. Many bright colours are used.

Height: 8¼ inches
Printed: Godden's Elsmore and Forster mark no. **477**

167
Giraffe
Burgess and Leigh
March 23, 1864
RD No. 172876

On this orange enamelled earthenware jug a long neck giraffe stands eating from a tree branch. There is an unusual orange peel background and a tree branch handle.

Height: 9 inches

Embossed:
Registration diamond
From the Cameron Hall Collection

A white stippled stoneware jug, more bulbous than many of the Brownfield designs. Strapwork forms highly stylized flowers and dividers over the bowl and around the neck. Also found in white with colored enamel ground.

Height: 8½ inches
Embossed: Brownfield's double circle bearing the words **"Tyrol," Cobridge** and the initials **W.B.**

169
"Florence"

William Brownfield
April 1, 1865
RD No. 185520

A white stoneware jug with metal lid, flat rim and white handle. Double blue vertical stripes alternate with white ones around the bowl, and a triple blue ring surrounds the neck.

Height: 6¾ inches
Embossed: A circular band bearing the impressed initials **W.B.**, the size number **30** and the words **Cobridge** and **"Florence."**
Embossed inside the ring: Registration diamond

168
"Tyrol"

William Brownfield
Oct. 12, 1864
RD No. 179656

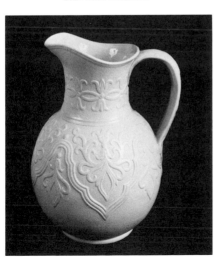

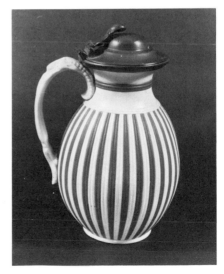

170
Wheatsheaf

Edward F. Bodley & Co.
June 29, 1865
RD No. 187847

A white, stippled stoneware jug with a large wheatsheaf, very like the Dudson wheatsheaf, on each side. There are sprigs of wheat behind the handle and down the front bridging the seam of the jug and a leaf border at the bottom.

Height: 8¾ inches
Embossed: Registration diamond
Embossed: Ribbon with an indistinguishable word or initials within (probably representing the name of the potter or the retailer.)

171
Strapwork

J. Edwards & Son
July 12, 1865
RD No. 188167

A white stippled stoneware jug with deep burgundy trim at the neck rim and around the neck. Strapwork of simulated metal bands separate various types of stylized leaves. Strapwork also surrounds the neck.

Height: Unknown
Embossed: Registration diamond
Embossed: Ribbon containing registration number **188167**
Printed: Circular metal band stating:
Ironstone China
J. Edwards and Son
Dale Hall
Printed: **839**

172
"Argyle"

James Dudson
Registered Dec. 23, 1865
RD No. 193844

A grey-green stippled stoneware jug with an argyle pattern covering the bowl, headed by a band of beading. The neck is covered with an acanthus leaf. Dudson also made an all over "Argyle" pattern. (See Hughes number 193 Book II).

Height: Unknown
Embossed: Ring bearing the words **Hanley and Argyle**, the number **10,**

and the initials believed to be **E.N.** and **T.A.C.,** probably the retailer's initials. This mark was also used on Argyle wares after 1865.

Identified by Mrs. Derek Dudson
From the Morpeth Collection

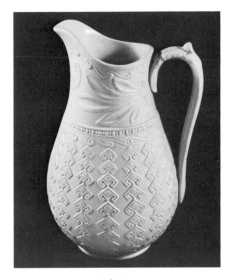

173
"Portland Vase"

Adams
c. 1865

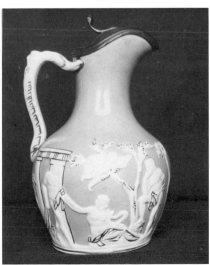

Another version of the "Portland Vase" motif which was popular in the mid-eighteen hundreds. This one is stoneware with a pink glaze and white figures. The handle is outlined in gold. The metal lid is marked T. Booth and Co. Compare to Hughes #56, Book 1, the Alcock version.

Height: 8 inches
Printed: **Adams**
Lid engraved: **T. Booth and Co.**
From the W.J. Rees Collection

174
"Universe"

William Brownfield
c. 1865

This jug bears figures in cartouches, representing four continents: Asia, Africa, America and Europe. At the handle is a map of the Eastern Hemisphere, on the front a map of the Western Hemisphere.

Height: 7¼ inches
Embossed: Brownfield knot with W.B. and a 6 impressed within

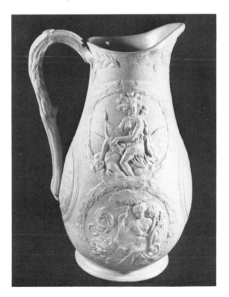

A stippled stoneware jug typical of the mid-1860's, with fern fronds and long pointed leaves covering the bowl. A leaf follows the contour of the rim and lip.

Height: Unknown
Unmarked
Authenticated by Mrs. Derek Dudson
Courtesy of the Derek Dudson Family

Embossed: Ribbon with **"Universe"** impressed within
From the Morpeth Collection

175
"Fern Fronds"
James Dudson
c. 1865

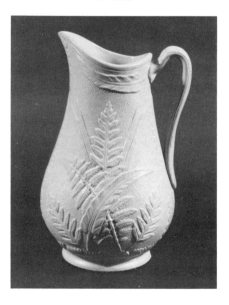

176
Hops, Wheat and Vine
James Dudson
c. 1865

A dark blue tankard stoneware jug which has been thrown, then sprigged, with white clusters of grapevines, hops vines and wheat separated by 4 broken columns. There is a high body weight and a very small foot-rim.

Height: 6¼ inches
Incised: **655**
Identified by Mrs. Derek Dudson

177
Classical
Old Hall Earthenware Company, Ltd.
c. 1865

A blue stoneware jug with four classical

medallions in white surrounding the bowl. The neck is ridged.

Height: 6½ inches
Embossed: Rosette with **O.H.E.C.L.**
From the W.J. Rees Collection

Eight vertical rows of overlapping and graduated shells surround the entire bowl of this parian jug. These are separated by elongated, stylized plant leaves. The background is blue with white decoration.

Height: 7¾ inches
Unmarked
From the Cameron Hall Collection

179
"The Volunteer Rifle Corps"
Unknown
c. 1855

Two soldiers, probably of Crimean war vintage, with rifle in hand, stand full length on this white stoneware jug. The background is an unusual all over pattern of tiny teardrops. The ribbon around the spout says, "The Volunteer Rifle Corps."

178
Sea Shells
Unknown
c. 1865

Height: 8 inches
Impressed: **No 2**

180
Fishwives

J & MP Bell
Glasgow, Scotland
May 6, 1867
Registration #207938

A cream earthenware jug with figures painted in natural colors. It is a very late piece to bear a genre design. On one side a medieval housewife buys fish from a fisherman. On the reverse she meets and visits with another wife who is also bearing home her purchases. Under the spout is inscribed, "Mrs. D. Scott, 1867," obviously a lady for whom the jug was made.

Height: 7½ inches
Embossed and Impressed: Registration Diamond inside a circle with **J & MP Bell, Glasgow** inside
From the Cameron Hall Collection

181
"Caterer"

Josiah Wedgwood
June 6, 1867
Reg. No. 208750

A multi colored, tankard shaped, majolica jug designed for Wedgwood by F.B. Russel. In four bands around the bowl is moulded, "WHAT THO' MY GATES BE POOR/TAKE THEM IN GOOD PART/BETTER CHEER YOU MAY HAVE/BUT NOT WITH BETTER HEART." Between these four bands are three rows of turquoise ovals. Colors are tur-

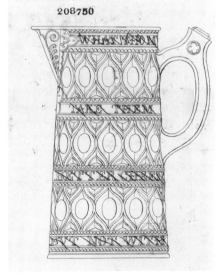

quoise, brown, dark blue and tan.

Height: 7⅞
Impressed: **Wedgwood**

*From the Design Registration Books in the
Public Records Office #208750*

182
Arches and Medallions

G.L. Ashworth & Bros.
September 21, 1867
RD No. 211536

A white stippled stoneware jug decorated with bands of medallions and
arches which are coloured with green
and red enamels. A very bright colour-
ful jug.

Height: 8¾ inches
Embossed: Registration diamond
Impressed: **Ashworth**
Impressed: **19**
Painted in red: **B151**

183
Hops Jug

Powell and Bishop
October 31, 1867
RD No. 213065

A white stoneware jug with a dark
brown stippled ground, encircled by a
freely growing hops vines. Overlapping leaves form a border at the
base; fluting surrounds the neck.

Height: 8¼ inches
Embossed: Registration diamond
Painted in brown: **4178**

184
Putti

Minton
May 8, 1845
RD No. 27451

A large blue and white parian jug with
a tree branch handle which has on the
sides of the bowl two cupids in very
deep relief picking hops berries. Hops
vines cover the bowl. The heads and
some parts of the bodies of the cupids
have been moulded and later applied.
Bennington also produced this design,
reportedly copied from a Wedgwood

jug. It is illustrated in Mr. Barrett's book on Bennington pottery. This jug was originally registered on May 8, 1845, however this particular piece was produced in 1868.

Height: 7 inches
Impressed: **Minton** and year cipher for 1868
From the W.J. Rees Collection

185
"Severn"

William Brownfield
June 19, 1869
RD No. 230184

A white stoneware jug with dark blue stippled ground at the neck, middle of the bowl and on the small foot-rim. A white band of fish netting is at the neck and on the bottom of the bowl, while a very large fish net design circles the waist. There is a rope handle.

Height: 6 inches
Embossed: Brownfield circle with a registration diamond in the middle
Impressed in the circle: **W.B., Severn, 24, Cobridge**

186
"Nile"

William Brownfield
June 10, 1870
RD No. 242392

A blue stippled stoneware jug with a prominent white Greek key design at the neck and around the bowl, and a stylized leaf design around the middle. There is a band of vitruvian scroll (Running Dog) design at the flat top lip, and a white angular handle.

Height: 6¾ inches
Embossed: A circular band bearing the impressed words: **Nile, and Cobridge,** and the initials **W.B.**
Embossed: Registration diamond

187
Marsh Marigold

W.T. Copeland & Sons
July 15, 1870
RD No. 243207

A white stoneware jug with flat rim, low handle and high body weight and a missing flat metal lid. This very stylized flower may be a marsh marigold. There is a wheel-like design around the neck.

Height: Unknown
Impressed: **Copeland**
From the Morpeth Collection

189
"Muses"

James Dudson
Registered by Joseph Parker
of 19 Ely Place, Holborn
November 21, 1870
RD No. 247901

A blue jasper thrown jug which has been sprigged with seven classical muses in various poses. They seem to be as follows: the pensive Polymnia, muse of hymn or song; Terpsichore with her lyre, muse of choral dance; Clio with scroll, muse of history; Euterpe with pipes, muse of lyric poetry; Urania with globe, muse of astronomy; and Calliope with book, muse of epic poetry. These figures stand on a border of roundels and dividers. There is a very delicate border of acanthus leaves and beading on the neck, and underneath is a modified egg and dart border. The quality of the jasper is extremely fine and smooth as is the quality of the sprigging. It is interesting to note that this jug was registered with the patent office under the number 247901 by a Joseph Parker of 19 Ely Place, Holborn, most likely a retailer or wholesaler of ceramics. Number 19 Ely Place was until the turn of the century located in a row of Georgian houses which were torn down at that time to build a large modern building.

188
"Hampton"

William Brownfield
June 12, 1868
RD No. 219316

There are white grape leaves surrounding a brown stippled body and a grapevine handle.

Height: 5⅝ inches
Impressed: **W.B., Hampton, Cobridge** in a circle
Impressed: Registration diamond

It is most unlikely that a pottery could have been located there according to the Vicar of the Church nearby. The design of this jug is a Dudson pattern and was most likely produced by that company.

Height: 7 inches
Incised: **1152** (pattern number)
Impressed: **24**
Impressed: **W**
Impressed: **L**
Identified by Mrs. Derek Dudson

190
Foxglove and Fern
William Ridgway
c. 1870

A yellowish tan stoneware jug with foxglove and fern surrounding a stippled bowl. This piece is tankard shaped and should date circa 1870 even though the mark on the bottom says otherwise. It is obvious that the early Ridgway Published by mark of 1835 used on the Tam-o-Shanter jug has been used again on a much later piece.

Height: 7½ inches
Impressed: **Published by William Ridgway & Co Hanley Oct. 1, 1835**

191
"Sisyphus"
William Brownfield
c. 1870

A blue stoneware tankard with an unusual heavy two-tiered base. Under the flat lip is a band of ivy on stippling, then a band of grooves and reeds. There is a C shaped handle.

Height: Unknown
Impressed: Godden's Brownfield mark number **666**
Impressed: Ribbon bearing **SISYPHUS 30**

192
"Acanthus and Bluebell"*

James Dudson
c. 1870

A blue jasper coated stoneware tankard which has been thrown and sprigged with upright white fern fronds alternating with white snowdrop sprigs. There is a rope handle. Also found is a white stoneware sugar bowl.

Height: Unknown
Unmarked
Courtesy of the Derek Dudson Family
* Dudson called this pattern "Acanthus and Blue Bell"

193
"Argyle"

James Dudson
c. 1870

A white stoneware jug with an all-over argyle pattern on a stippled background. Also found with a background of alternating dark blue, green and rust. (See Hughes number 172, Book II)

Height: 8½ inches
Unmarked
Identified by Mrs. Derek Dudson

193a

An enamelled version of Dudson's argyle pattern

194
"Boston"

James Dudson
c. 1891

A stoneware jug, fairly straight-sided with two tiers and a very small foot-rim. Four stylized medallions surround each tier topped by a flat rim and a pointed fluted spout.

Height: Unknown
Unmarked
Identified by Mrs. Derek Dudson
Courtesy of the Derek Dudson Family

195
"Fern Wreath"

James Dudson
c. 1870

A blue jasper coated white stoneware jug with a Dudson rope handle and a tankard shape. It has been thrown, then sprigged with a band of various fern fronds around the middle.

Height: 6¼ inches
Incised: **1043***

Impressed: **24**
Impressed: **L**
Impressed: **O**
* On another jug of this pattern is the incised number 1277. Different numbers would have been used if one jug was jasper and one was jasper coated.

196
"Jewel"

James Dudson
c. 1870

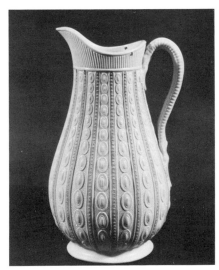

A tall stippled tan and white stoneware jug with vertical chains of stylized jewels separated by rows of beading. Gadrooning rings the neck and high spout, and there is a small foot-rim. This is another press-moulded jug which has been sprigged.

Height: Unknown
Authenticated by Mrs. Derek Dudson
Courtesy of the Derek Dudson Family

197
"Convolvulus"

James Dudson
c. 1860

A white stoneware tankard jug with stylized morning glories on a fence.

Height: 7 inches
Unmarked
This jug identified by Mrs. Derek Dudson
From the Morpeth Collection

A pale stoneware jug with a waisted tankard shape. Hops vines encircle the neck, while stylized acanthus leaves cover the bowl. There is fluting on the high pointed spout.

Height: Unknown
Identified by Mrs. Derek Dudson
Courtesy of the Derek Dudson Family

199
"Can't You Talk?"

Unknown
c. 1870

198
"Scroll"

James Dudson
c. 1870

A highly glazed stoneware jug with pink ground and white figures, handle and inside. On each side a small child on hands and knees talks to a big white dog who looks totally puzzled. The caption reads, "Can't You Talk?". The top and bottom of the jug bear a barrel design.

Height: 6¾ inches
Umarked

200
Fern and Rope

Unknown
c. 1870

A white stippled stoneware jug with flat lip and small foot-rim. Large fern fronds grow upright around the bowl separated by a rope which goes around the neck and the foot-rim, and down the handle.

Height: Unknown
Unmarked
From the Morpeth Collection

A tan stoneware modified tankard jug with a stippled background. There are four cartouches each of which contain a stylized bird sitting in grapevines. The bird handle is most interesting as the bird, complete with feathers, appears to be swallowing the top end of the handle.

Height: 9⅜ inches
Impressed: ✿

201
Oak Leaf and Acorns

Unknown
c. 1870

200a
Bird in Grapevines

Unknown
c. 1870

A large white late Victorian stoneware jug with oak leaves and acorns all around the bowl. There is a tree trunk handle and stippling all over the body.

Height: 9⅞ inches
Unmarked

202
Fluted Tankard

Unknown
c. 1870

A very straight sided tankard in white stoneware with deep recessed strips around the bowl. There is a small band of stylized acanthus leaves at the neck, and a border of egg-like shapes at the base. The lip is unusually high-flaring for the period.

Height: Unknown
Unmarked
From the Morpeth Collection

203
Gamekeeper

Unknown
c. 1870

A white parian jug with ivy leaves

around the neck and the figure of a kneeling game keeper on each side of the bowl. Multicoloured enamels highlight the design. Similar to a marked example by T. Booth, Hanley.

Height: 3 inches
Printed: Painters mark
From the W. J. Rees Collection

204
Stylized Leaves

Unknown
c. 1870

Stylized leaves surround the bowl of a white stippled stoneware jug, on top and bottom of which runs a deep rust

81

coloured scalloped edging. Above and below these edgings is a band of rust. The Prince of Wales' feathers are inside a continuous figure eight ring at the neck and foot.

Height: 7¾ inches
Unmarked

205
Swan
Unknown
c. 1870

A white parian jug with a swan in a niche on both front and back. Beautiful quality moulding.

Height: 4 inches
Unmarked
From the W.J. Rees Collection

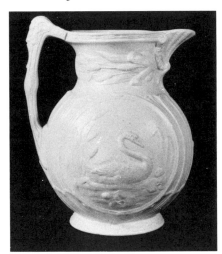

206
Teardrop
Unknown
c. 1870

A white stoneware jug with flat rim, angular handle and a very low body weight. A ring of decoration around the bowl looks like many jewels hang-

ing from a necklace. This motif is repeated in a diamond shape around the neck. The spout is fluted.

Height: Unknown
Unmarked
From the Morpeth Collection

207
Turkey Oak
Unknown
c. 1870

A mustard coloured flat-rimmed

stoneware jug with a tree trunk handle
which ends on the bowl in a large
branch of turkey oak leaves and nuts.

Height: Unknown
Unmarked
From the Morpeth Collection

208
Bird and Butterfly
Brownhills Pottery Co.
c. 1875

A light blue thrown stoneware jug
which has been sprigged with a white
butterfly amid ferns on one side and a
large white bird on a branch on the
reverse. There is a moulded handle.
This identical jug was made by Dudson. While there is an impressed B.P. &
Co. on the bottom, there is also the
incised pattern number in the style
used by Dudson. Dudson probably
made this jug for Brownhills. Mrs.
Derek Dudson says that this was some-
times done.

Height: 5¾ inches
Incised: **3532½**
Impressed: **BP & Co.**
Impressed: **A**
Impressed: **V**

209
"Tropical Bird"
James Dudson
c. 1875

A dark ground stoneware tankard with metal lid and tree branch handle. The bowl is covered with bamboo shoots in which sits a large bird with a very long pointed beak.

Height: Unknown
Identified by Mrs. Derek Dudson
Courtesy of the Derek Dudson Family

210
Barrel and Rope
Probably Ridgway
c. 1875

A white stoneware tankard jug with a purple rope handle which continues around the neck of the jug. White barrel stays compose the top, jagged pineapple-like leaves make up the bottom of the piece.

Height: Unknown
Unmarked
Also found in green with a Ridgway "Published by" mark and dated October 1, 1835. Obviously an earlier mark has been used on a later design.
From the Morpeth Collection

211
Empty Cartouche

Pinder Bourne & Co.
September 6, 1876
RD No. 303308

A tall brown stippled stoneware tankard with over-all Tudor strapwork design in which an empty cartouche is centered. There is a guilloche border at the top and bottom and a missing flat metal lid.

Height: Unknown
Embossed: Registration diamond
From the Morpeth Collection

212
Stylized Floral

James Edwards & Son
July 17, 1877
RD No. 312020

Highly stylized flowers are arranged on a white stippled stoneware body. There are two border designs at the neck, and one on the foot-rim. The design for this jug was registered by James Edwards & Son as found in the design registration books. However, the only mark on the bottom is not identified.

Height: Unknown
Embossed: Ribbon bearing the initials **CAM**
From the Morpeth Collection

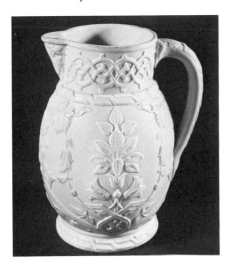

213
Bird in Bamboo

F. & R. Pratt and Co.
October 24, 1877
RD No. 315574

A tankard style stoneware jug with metal lid. It has a brown stippled background on which a bird and butterfly are shown in shallow relief among bamboo stalks. Bright enamels have been used to highlight the relief.

Height: 8 inches
Impressed: Registration diamond
Impressed: **F.R.P. & Co.**
From the W.J. Rees Collection

214
"Brent"

James Dudson
July, 1878

A small thrown, straight-sided, brown stoneware cream jug on a small foot-rim. There is a white band toward the base on which stand sprigged figures as follows: a muse holding a wreath and a bird, a modestly dressed putto, a lyre, tree and flowers, the rear view of another putto holding a bow, and a muse holding a branch and a small hanging vessel. Beneath the handle is a roundel.

Height: 3½ inches
Incised: **1360**
Impressed: **Brent**
Impressed: **M**
Impressed: **30**
Impressed: **7**
78
Impressed: The four Dudson dots i.e. .
. .

215
Toucan

F. & R. Pratt & Co.
January 16, 1879
Registration Number: 331342

A most unusual blue stoneware jug
with a black stippled enamelled background. On each side a large Toucan
sits on a palm branch above a Greek key
fretwork design. There is a gold band
at the top rim and around the bottom.

Height: 5⅝ inches
Incised: Registration Diamond
Incised: **F&RP & Co.**
Embossed: **30**
From the Tim Sublette Collection

216
Independence

Unknown
c. 1880

This white stoneware jug bears the
bust of George Washington in a olive
leaf draped cartouche with a ribbon
underneath containing the word
Washington. Above, it says Born Feb.
22, 1732. On the reverse are two
crossed American flags containing 13
stars each. Above the flags is incised
Independence 1776. This is probably a
commemorative piece put out about
1876 and could well be American
instead of English.

Height: 7⅛ inches
Unmarked

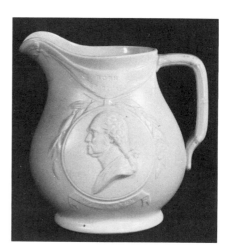

217
"Montana"

William Brownfield
August 25, 1883
RD No. 402839

This is a diamond shaped tankard in
grey-green stoneware. Rose-like flowers are spotted all over the three

dimensional herringbone pattern background. There is an angular handle and small diamond shaped footrim.

Height: Unknown
Embossed: Godden's Brownfield mark number **66**
Embossed: Registration diamond
Embossed: Ribbon with **Montana 30** impressed
Impressed: **M**
Impressed: **4/84** (production date)

218
Good Ale
Doulton & Co. (Ltd.)
1884

The Doulton jugs are a study in themselves as there are hundreds of interesting designs, but this one example will be included as a point of reference. A tan and brown stoneware jug has been thrown, then sprigged, with four pinwheel designs and the following saying around the pinwheels: "He that buys land buys stones, he that buys flesh buys bones, he that buys eggs buys many shells, he that buys good ale buys nothing else."

Height: 6¾ inches
Impressed: Godden's Doulton mark number **1329**
Impressed: **1884**
Impressed: **600**

219
"Topers"
W.T. Copeland
c. 1885

The pub scene on this tankard jug is taken from a Flemish painting by Ten-

Impressed: **WUP** (date letters for August 1887)

niers. On each side of a grey-green stoneware jug is a group of peasants sitting, smoking and drinking in a pub. It is heavily stippled with multiple bands of design at the top and the bottom. It once had a metal lid. The handle is in the shape of a squared-off capital C. This is a thrown and sprigged jug.

Height: Unknown
Impressed: **Copeland**
Impressed: **36**
Impressed: ☐
From the Morpeth Collection

220a

White Phrygian head applied to the bottom of jug number 220, Book II
From the John and Linda Dohmlo Collection

220
"Portland Vase"
Josiah Wedgwood
August 1887

A Wedgwood replica of the Portland Vase in light blue jasperware and white sprigging. (See Hughes jug number 56, Book 1, for an Alcock example.) Applied to the bottom of the jug is a white Phrygian head. (See Hughes number 220a Book II).

Height: 5½ inches
Impressed: **Wedgwood**
Impressed: **M**

221
"Etruscan Jug"

Josiah Wedgwood
1890

Between two wide borders of white classical design are found: white sprigged female figures, a pedestal on which stands an angel, a pedestal holding a fire. Also there are urns, flowers and trees. A blue ground has been used on a thrown stoneware body. The little metal lid has a porcelain knob opening device.

Height: 7 inches
Impressed: **Wedgwood**
Impressed: **S** (year symbol for 1890)
Impressed: **England**
Impressed: **24**

222
Mask and Dolphin
Unknown
c. 1890

A highly glazed blue earthenware jug designed in the style of the 1840's with large foot-rim, high flaring spout and a high dolphin head handle. A Viking mask is on either side of the bowl, and a large satyr mask sits beneath the spout. Stylized acanthus and grape

leaves make this a very ornate jug. It is from this example that the modern Mask and Dolphin jug was copied. (See Hughes number 202, Book 1).

Height: 8½ inches
Unmarked

223
Boar and Stag Hunt
G.L. Ashworth & Bros.
c. 1891

It would appear that the original mould for the Mason's jug (Hughes number 55, Book I, Boar and Stag Hunt), was used after 1891 for this

highly glazed revival. The leaves are in bright orange and green, the animals in gold, grey and beige, all on a heavy yellow glaze. The body is stoneware.

Height: 8 inches
Printed in black: Godden's Masons mark no. **2530**
Printed in red: **K**

224
The Diamond Jubilee
Unknown
1897

A cream and tan colored stoneware jug commemorating the Diamond Jubilee celebration for Queen Victoria in 1897. On one side of the jug is a bust of the young Victoria in an oval cartouche. On the other side we see her as an old lady. A banner above her head on both sides bears the dates June 20, 1837 and June 20, 1897. Underneath the busts, a banner says, "Cum pace vent" and "Cum honore vici," or, "I come with peace, I conquer with honor." Down the front and back of the jug, around the neck and base and down the handle runs a garland of the traditional emblems of the various countries comprising the British Isles, that is: the rose of England, the shamrock of Ireland and the thistle of Scot-

land. Strangely, the three feathers of Wales are not on the garland.

Height: **7** inches
Unmarked

225
"Empress"
J. Dimmock & Co.
c. 1897

A very plain white stoneware tankard with a pair of bands at the top, middle and bottom. There is a very interesting elephant with tusk handle. It is likely that this jug called, "Empress," by J. Dimmock and Co. was so named in commemoration of the coronation of Queen Victoria as Empress of India in 1897.

Height: Unknown
Embossed: A large circle containing a six point star. The letters spelling **Empress** are between each point of the star, and the number **12** is in the middle.
Embossed under circle: Rectangle with **J.D. & Co.** impressed
Impressed: **76**
Impressed: **11**

226
Durbar
Unknown
c. 1897

A heavily glazed grey-green stoneware jug with an angular handle. The jug stands on six feet. A royal procession consisting of a carriage pulled by two elephants and another carriage pulled by two camels surround the bowl. This jug was probably made to commemorate the crowning of Queen Victoria as Empress of India in 1897. In 1876 Parliament, under the guidance of Disralli, passed the law which made her Empress of India. This jug and the one above could have been produced at that time.

Height: 7 inches
Unmarked

227
Hunt
Copeland Late Spode
c. 1900

This is a tan stoneware turn-of-the-century copy of an earlier hunting scene jug. It is thrown and sprigged with three hunters and horses, who approach a fallen stag being killed by five dogs. There is a stylized border at the top and bottom.

Height: 5½ inches
Printed: Godden's Copeland Late Spode mark number **1076**
Printed: **No. 180288**
Impressed: **England, Copeland**

228
Mermaid and Cupid
Minton
1911

A most unusual celedon green and white parian jug with a very deep and well moulded relief. On the side a large

cupid swings on ivy vines which are attached to a horned mask in the center of the front of the jug. There is an extended bowl under the handle on which sits the full figure of a lovely mermaid. The shape (without figures) for this jug was registered in 1844, and the design was produced for many years. It copied a wine ewer excavated at Pompeii and is also found in majolica in the Minton Museum. The figures and mask are applied.

Height: 6 inches
Impressed: **Minton**
Incised: **1420** (Minton ornament design number)
Impressed: Year cypher for 1911
Courtesy of the Minton Musuem

229
Hops
Boehm, USA
c. 1950

A plain white parian jug in the 19th century style with hops vines at the top and at the base of the handle. This is a 20th century American copy of a 19th

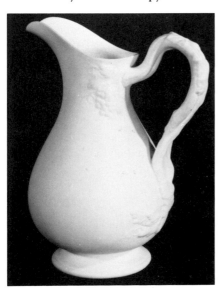

century jug and was made by the famous Boehm company.

Height: 8⅜ inches
Printed: **Boehm, USA**

230
"Basket"
Dudson Bros. Ltd.
1975

A white stoneware jug limited to an edition of 500 pieces produced in 1975 to commemorate the 175th anniversary of the Dudson Company. These reproduction jugs were made from moulds taken from a 19th century Dudson jug. The design is an overall basket weave pattern.

Height: 7 inches
Printed in black:
Dudson Jug
Manufactured from the original
mould used to produce the
specimen exhibited in the
Victoria and Albert Museum
London, England
Made in England
Limited edition of 500
Number 135

231
"Grape"
Portmeirion Pottery, Ltd.
1984

Portmeirion Pottery have recently reproduced a number of designs of Victorian jugs from the original moulds. Even without the mark on the bottom of the jug, however, one would know that this example is a reproduction because of the rougher feel of the body. The moulding, on the other hand, is beautifully reproduced. Portmeirion calls this jug, "Grape." It is a copy of the Hops jug, Hughes number 151, Book II.

Height: 8½ inches
Printed:

**Portmeirion
Pottery**

**Stoke-on-Trent
Made in England**

232
Resting Putti
Unknown
20th century

A twentieth century copy of Hughes jug number 95, Book 1, Resting Putti. On each side of a white highly glazed stoneware jug is a sleeping putto surrounded by roses and flowers. A bank of gadrooning surrounds the bottom of the bowl.

Height: 9 inches
Unmarked

233

The following are a group of moulded wares other than jugs:

233a
Bacchus
Unknown
c. 1790

A Pratt type mug on which the head of a bearded Bacchus covers the bowl.

Height: 3½ inches
Unmarked

233b
Mandarin Tea Pot
Unknown
c. 1830

A very ornate stoneware pot with a Chinese Mandarin head flanked by pelicans on the bowl. The spout is the head of a fish; the finial of the lid is a seashell; the handle is a tree branch; and the whole design is put together with many scrolls and flourishes.

Height: Unknown
Unmarked
From the Morpeth Collection

233c
Pan Mustard Pot
William Ridgway
1832

A small tan stoneware mustard pot with silver lid bearing the design of Bacchus and scrolls. (See Hughes jug no. 14, Book 1). On this example Pan has been left off the handle.

Height: 3 inches
Engraved on the lid: Silver marks for 1832

233d
Gadrooned Teapot
William Ridgway, Son & Co.
1838

An extremely low tan stoneware pot with gadrooning around the top and bottom divided by a plain band. Gadrooning also surrounds the knop on the ceramic lid. There is a high-rising handle. This would seem to be William Ridgway, Son & Co.'s. pattern number one.

Height: Unknown
Impressed: **W. Ridgway, Son & Co.**
Impressed: **1**
From the Morpeth Collection

233e
Bamboo and Flowers Tea Pot

James Dudson
c. 1845

In each of six large cartouches on the bowl of this stoneware tea pot is an arrangement of leaves and stylized flowers. Areas between the cartouches are stippled. The lid bears three of these cartouches and a rose head finial. On the bowl and spout are bamboo stalks. An unusual feature of this tea pot is that it was moulded, not thrown, then sprigged.

Height: Unknown
Incised: **104** and **36**
Identified by Mrs. Derek Dudson
From the Morpeth Collection

233f
Waterlily Candlestick

W.T. Copeland
c. 1850

A lovely white parian candlestick in Copeland's Waterlily pattern. (See Hughes jug number 103, Book 1). Ivy leaves surround the neck, and waterlily leaves wind around the base of the candlestick.

Height: 8¾ inches
Impressed: **Copeland**
Impressed: **3**

233g
Butter Tub and Plate

Samuel Alcock & Co.
c. 1845

An Alcock lavender stoneware butter tub, complete with lid and under plate. A well modelled white cow rests on the lid as a finial.

Height: 4 inches
Printed: Godden's Alcock Royal Arms mark, Godden's number **78**
Printed: **128**

233h
"John Barleycorn" Cheese Dish
William Ridgway & Co.
c. 1856

A large white stoneware cheese dish in the Ridgway "John Barleycorn" pattern of hops vines on strapwork. (See Hughes number 133, Book 1). This piece is unmarked, but the pattern is identical to the marked jug.

Height: 12 inches
Unmarked

Printed: Godden's Copeland Late Spode mark **No. 1076.**
Printed: **England**
Impressed: **Copeland, England**
Impressed: RD 285413 (Date for Sept. 1874, not the date of Production of the jug.)
Impressed: **36**

233j
"Dancing" Jardiniere
James Dudson
c. 1900

A dark blue jasper coated stoneware jardiniere which has been thrown, then sprigged with the classical Houri, or Dancing Hours. Side-by-side rosettes ring the neck.

Height: Unknown
Authenticated by Mrs. Derek Dudson
Courtesy of the Derek Dudson Family

233i
Jubilee Tea Pot
Copeland Late Spode
1897

A dark green, highly glazed, thrown stoneware jug with a white bust of an old Victoria on each side. Above and below the bust is a garland of roses, shamrocks, and thistles, which is also repeated on the lid. The tan finial is a crown, and the tan handle and spout are tree branches. On one side is Victoria's coat of arms. This tea pot was produced for her diamond jubilee.

Height: 5 inches

Digest of Public Records Office Jugs

In addition to the 400 odd patterns of 19th century Relief Moulded Jugs which have actually come to hand, there are many examples of jugs which were registered with the Public Records Office, but have not been actually found. The following list catalogs jugs found in and identified by the pictures in these wonderful books. Reference: Class IV, BT 43-65, 66, 67, 68, 69, and 70.

5994
Josiah Wedgwood
Mar. 21, 1843

31329
Herbert Minton & Co.
Nov. 22, 1845

55174
W.T. Copeland
Nov. 4, 1848

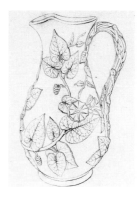

27586
T.J. & J. Mayer
May 1845

34108
Minton & Co.
March 2, 1846

63718
Minton & Co.
Nov. 17, 1849

80989
Wm. Brownfield
Oct. 16, 1851

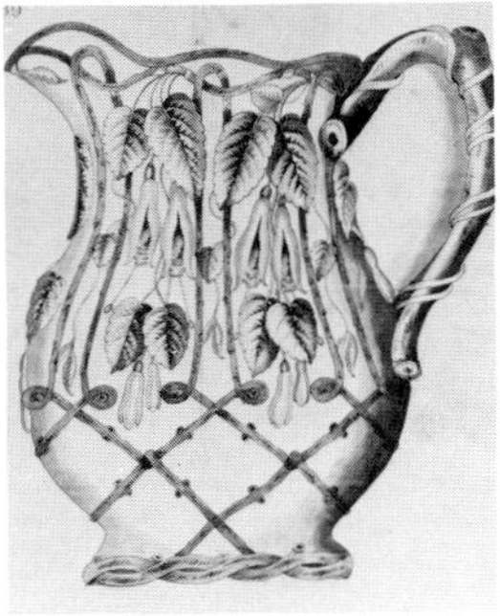

86657
Minton & Co.
Sept. 16, 1852

91405
Livelsey, Powell, and Co.
June 14, 1853

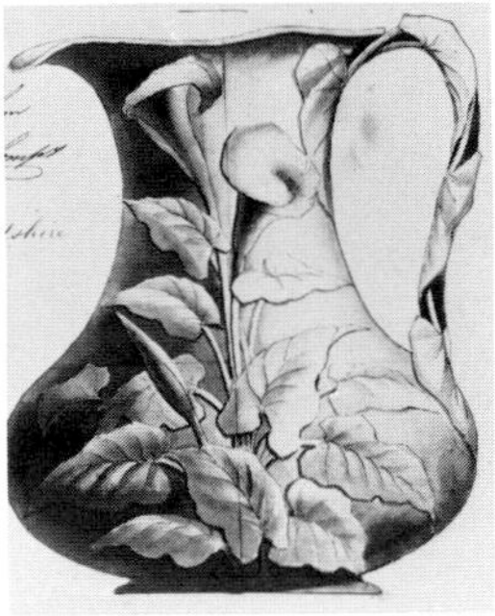

84471
J. & M.P. Bell & Co.
March 26, 1852

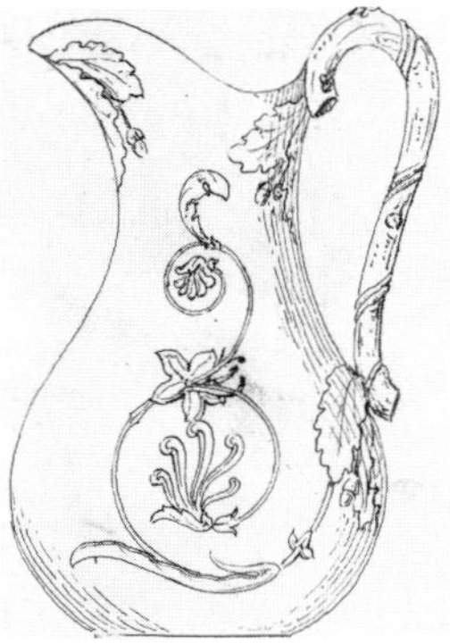

89646
Thos. Worthington & J. Green
Feb. 11, 1853

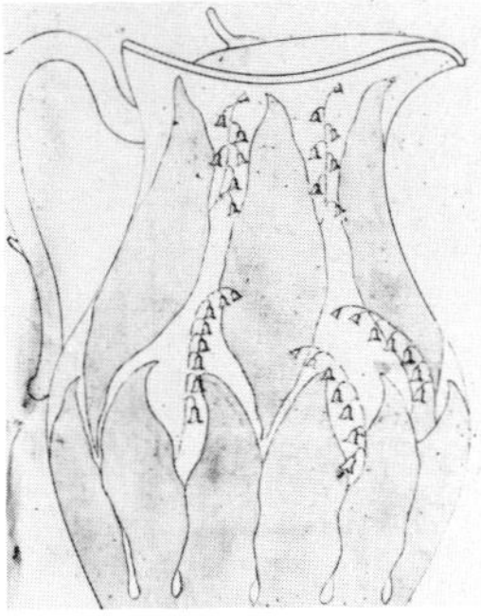

95163
W.T. Copeland
Feb. 23, 1854

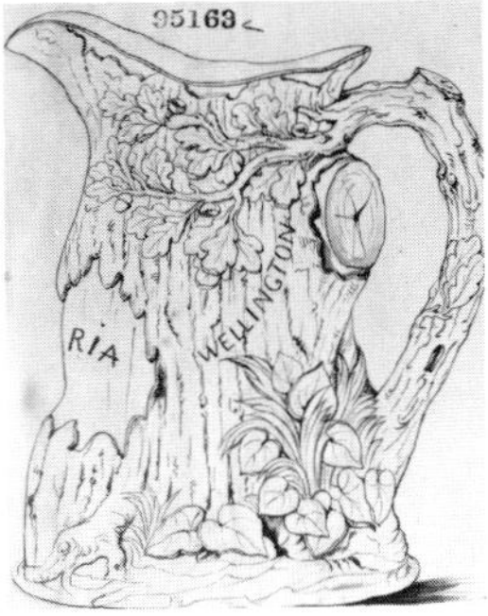

84541
Thos. Till & Son
April 1, 1852

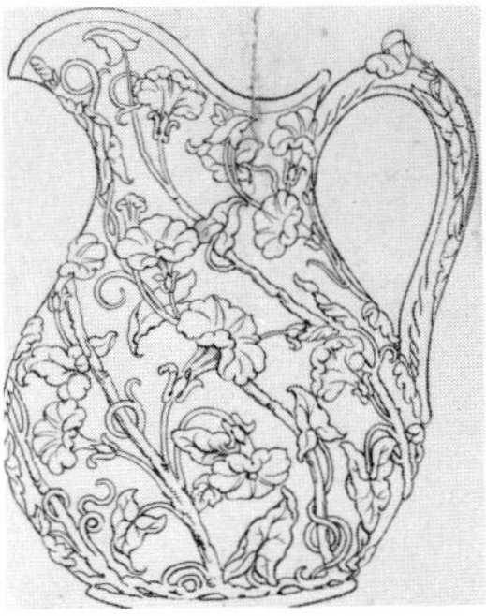

91329
Geo. Wood & Co.
June 7, 1853

95448
Geo. Baguley
Mar. 27, 1854

95451
J. Deaville
Mar. 27, 1854

99310
John Alcock
Feb. 7, 1855

99653
Warburton & Britton
Mar. 13, 1855

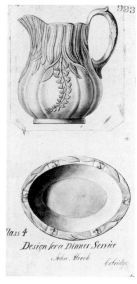

95510
Wm. Brownfield
Apr. 1, 1854

99086
Parkhurst & Dimmock
Jan. 19, 1855

99974
Wm. Brownfield
Apr. 26, 1855

101624
Samuel Bevington & Son
Sept. 27, 1855

103507
Minton & Co.
Jan. 23, 1856

105223
Worthington & Green
June 28, 1856

102785
Wm. Brownfield
Nov. 28, 1855

104603
Wm. Brownfield
Apr. 30, 1856

106770
W.T. Copeland
Oct. 22, 1856

103506
J. Roberts
Jan. 23, 1856

110161
Wilkinson & Rickhuss
June 19, 1857

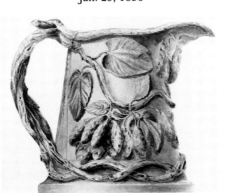

112354
Wm. Brownfield
Dec. 9, 1857

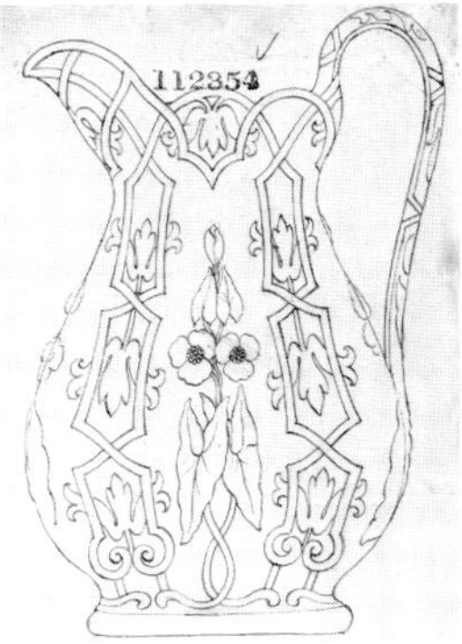

115120
Sharpe Bros. & Co.
Sept. 3, 1858

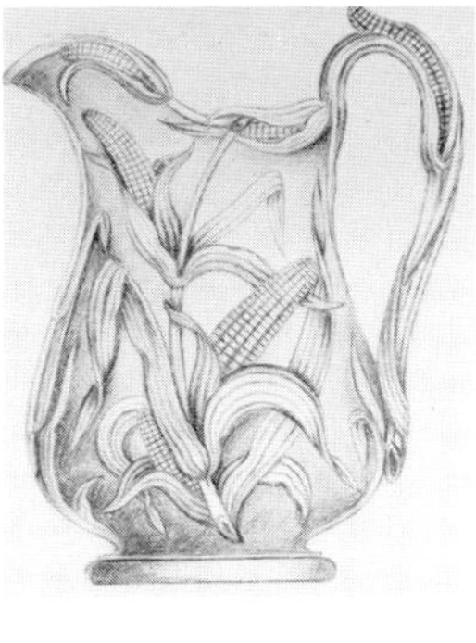

118891
T.R. Boote
Mar. 21, 1859

112876
E. & W. Walley
Jan. 29, 1858

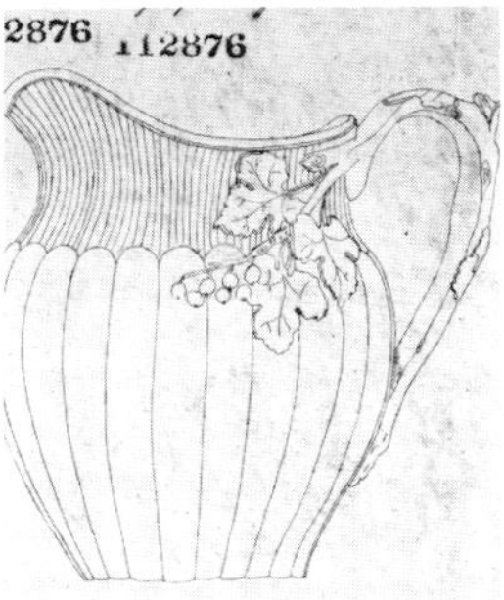

115902
Wm. Brownfield
Oct. 5, 1858

119721
E. & W. Walley
May 7, 1859

114532
Samuel Alcock & Co.
July 29, 1858

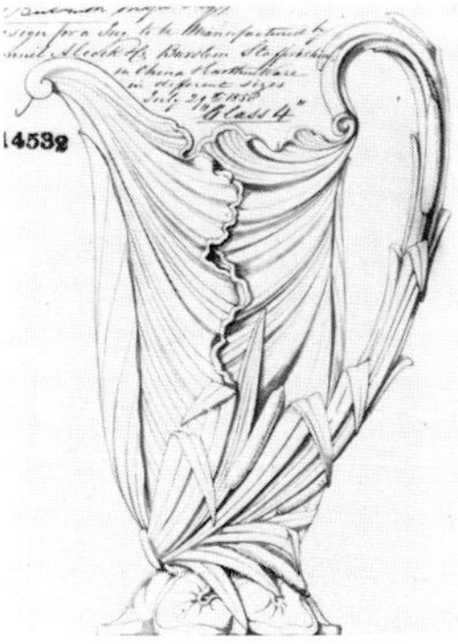

118415
Leveson Hill (Excrs. of)
Feb. 8, 1859

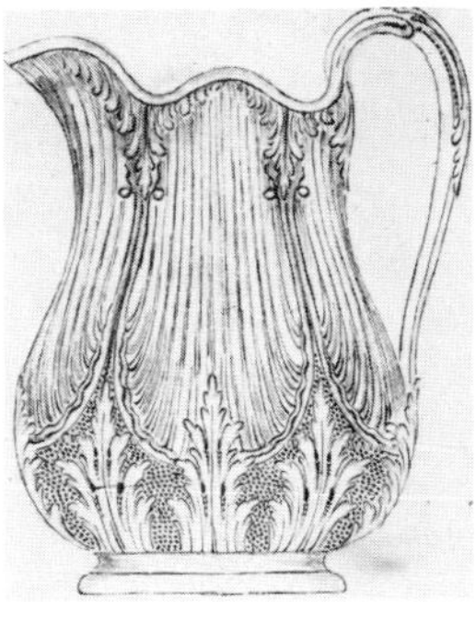

119722 E. & W. Walley
May 7, 1859

120096
Lockett, Baguley & Cooper
May 26, 1859

130462
Sanford Estate Clay Co. Ltd.
August 1860

131339
Sandford Estate Clay Co. Ltd.
July or Aug., 1860

129129
Lockett, Baguley & Cooper
May 19, 1860

130541
Sandford Estate Clay Co. Ltd.
June 1860

132167
Sandford Estate Clay Co. Ltd.
Aug. or Sept., 1860

130112
Sandford Estate Clay Co. Ltd.
June 1860

130542
Sandford Estate Clay Co. Ltd.
July or Aug., 1860

132168
Sandford Estate Clay Co. Ltd.
Aug. or Sept., 1860

134936
Minton & Co.
Oct. 29, 1860

139360
Pinder, Bourne & Hope
Apr. 5, 1861

141214
Bates, Brown, Westhead &
Moore
June 4, 1861

134968
Wm. Brownfield
Oct. 29, 1860

140480
The Old Hall Earthenware Co.
May 6, 1861

141727
Beech and Hancock
July 5, 1861

137529
Wedgwood & Co.
Jan. 21, 1861

140481
The Old Hall Earthenware Co.
May 6, 1861

141732
Wm. Brownfield
July 6, 1861

103

142847
Wedgwood & Co.
Aug. 22, 1861

149090
Elliot Bros.
Feb. 1, 1862

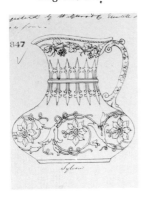

144896
Levenson Hill (Excrs. of)
Oct. 15, 1861

149673
James Dudson
Feb. 27, 1862

159123
Minton & Co.
Jan. 16, 1863

160457
Wilkinson & Sons
Mar. 13, 1863

146354
J. Clemenson
Nov. 15, 1861

149674
James Dudson
Feb. 27, 1862

161404
J. Macintyre
Apr. 11, 1863

170294
F. & R. Pratt & Co.
Dec. 18, 1863

1759 9
Wood & ~~ale~~
July 2, ~~~~ ~~4~~

162304
Harding & Cotterill
May 15, 1863

205088
John Meir & Son
Dec. 19, 1866

172060
Liddle, Elliot & Son
Feb. 25, 1864

168765
Wm. Kirkham
Nov. 16, 1863

212194
Thos. Booth
Oct. 10, 1867

237230
Belleek Pottery, Fermanagh,
Irel.
Dec. 18, 1869

256079
T.C. Brown, Westhead, Moore
& Co.
Sept. 25, 1871

260998
Bates, Elliot & Co.
Mar. 7, 1872

256907
W.T. Copeland & Sons
Oct. 19, 1871

265687
Bates, Elliot & Co.
Sept. 2, 1872

254030
Thos. Booth
July 15, 1871

259077
Edge Malkin & Co.
Jan. 1, 1872

266636
W.E. Cartlidge
Sept. 26, 1872

272835
T.C. Brown, Westhead, Moore
& Co.
May 12, 1873

289876
George Jones & Sons
March 12, 1875

301302
Josiah Wedgwood
June 19, 1876

273804
Pinder, Bourne & Co.
June 19, 1873

290352
Mintons
April 7, 1875

Reverse of Above

303942
Hope & Carter
Sept. 28, 1876

283275
Pinder, Bourne & Co.
June 16, 1874

294435
George Jones & Sons
Sept. 13, 1875

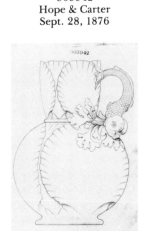

304128
Wm. Harrop
Oct. 7, 1876

311523
W.T. Copeland & Sons
July 2, 1877

318158
Geo. Jones
Jan. 30, 1878

319041
Dunn, Bennett & Co.
Mar. 9, 1878

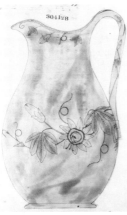

312187
Ford, Chillinor & Co.
July 25, 1877

304473
Edge, Malkin & Co.
Oct. 21, 1876

319296
Powell and Bishop
Mar. 9, 1878

310710
Joseph Holdcroft
June 7, 1877

314675
J. Holdcroft
Sept. 28, 1877

322168
F. Furnival & Sons
June 4, 1878

343148
Mintons
Nov. 21, 1879

362423
J. Dimmock & Co.
Mar. 3, 1881

351928
F.J. Emery
July 7, 1880

328018
The Brownhills Pottery Co.
Oct. 23, 1878

382859
Wright & Rigby
July 4, 1882

357560
Jones & Hopkinson
Oct. 30, 1880

333801
Clementson Bros.
Mar. 28, 1879

395818
E.A. Wood
Mar. 20, 1883

395819
Josiah Wedgwood & Sons
Mar. 20, 1883

403665
Josiah Wedgwood & Sons
Sept. 11, 1883

397819
S. Fielding & Co.
May 7, 1883

406371
S. Fielding & Co.
Nov. 1, 1883

Appendix I List of Potters

1. John Alcock
Cobridge, Staffs.
1853-1861
2. Samuel Alcock & Co. Cobridge
Hill Pottery, Burslem Staffor-
shire Potteries
c. 1828-1853
c. 1830-1859
c. 1828-1859
3. G.L. Ashworth & Bros.
Broad St.
Hanley, Staffs.
1862-
4. J.D. Bagster
High St., Hanley
Stoke-on-Trent, Staffs.
1823-1828
5. George Baguley
Hanley, Staffs.
6. Bates and Co. (perhaps J. Ridgway, Bates & Co.)
Cauldon Place, Staffordshire
Potteries Shelton, Hanley
Unknown
7. Bates, Brown, Westhead &
Moore
Cauldon Place
Shelton, Hanley
1859-1861
8. Bates Elliott & Co.
Dale Hall Works,
Burslem, Staffs.
1870-1875
9. Beech & Hancock
Church Bank Works
Swan Bank Pottery, Tunstall
Staffordshire Potteries
c. 1857-1861
c. 1862-1876
1857-1876
10. J. & M.P. Bell & Co.
Glasgow Pottery
Dobbies Loan
Glasgow, Scotland
1842-1928
11. Robert Bew of Bilston

Bilston
S. Yorkshire
1827-1851
12. John Bevington
Kensington Works
Hanley, Staffordshire
1872-1892
13. Samuel Bevington & Son
Burton Place Works
Hanley, Staffs.
Potted prior to 1865
14. Robert Bew
Bilston, S. Yorkshire
1827-1851
15. Edward F. Bodley & Co.
Scotia Pottery
Burslem, Staffs.
1862-1881
16. T. & R. Boote Ltd.
Waterloo Pottery
Burslem, Staffs.
1842-present
17. Thomas Booth
Turnstall, Staffs.
18. Bradbury, Anderson & Bettanny
Longdon, Staffordshire
1844-1852
19. T.C. Brown
Westhead Moore & Co.
Hanley
Unknown
20. William Brownfield & Son
Cobridge
Staffordshire
1850-1891
21. Brownhills Pottery Co.
Turnstall, Staffs.
1872-1896
22. Burgess & Leigh
Hill Pottery
Burslem, Staffs.
1867-1889
23. W.E. Cartlidge
Hanley, Staffs.
24. Clementson Bros. Ltd.

Phoenix Works and Bell Works
Hanley, Staffs.
1865-1916

25. Copeland & Garrett
Spode Works
Stoke, Staffordshire
1833-1847

26. W.T. Copeland
Spode Works
Stoke, Staffordshire
1847-present

27. Cork & Edge
Newport Pottery
Burslem, Staffordshire
1846-1860

28. Cork, Edge & Malkin
Newport Pottery
Burlsem, Staffordshire
1860-1871

29. H. & R. Daniels
London Rd.
Stoke-on-Trent, Staffs.
1820-1841

30. Davenport
Longport, Staffs.
1793-1887

31. J. Deaville
Hanley, Staffs.

32. J. Dimmock & Co.
Albion Works
Hanley, Staffordshire
Unknown

33. Doulton & Co. (Ltd.)
Nile St.
Burslem, Staffs.
1882-

34. James Dudson
Hope & Hanover Streets
Hanley, Staffordshire
1838-1888

35. Dudson Bros. Ltd.
Hope St.
Hanley, Staffs.
1898-

36. Dunn, Bennett & Co.
Royal Victorian Works
Burslem, Staffs.
1875-

37. James Edwards & Son

Dale Hall
Burslem, Staffs.
1851-1882

38. Elsmore & Forster
Clayhills Pottery
Tunstall, Staffs.
1853-1871

39. Edge, Malkin & Co. Ltd.
Newport and Middleport Potteries
Burslem, Staffs.
1871-1903

40. Elliot Bros.
Longport, Staffs.

41. F.J. Emery
Bleak Hill Works
Burslem, Staffs.
1878-1893

42. Ford, Challinor & Co.
(also listed as Ford and Challinor)
Lion Works
Sandyford, Tunstall, Staffs.
1865-1880

43. S. Fielding & Co.
Railway Pottery
Devon Pottery
Stoke-on-Trent, Staffs.
1879-

44. F. Furnival & Sons
Cobridge, Staffs.

45. Thomas Furnival & Co.
Miles Bank
Hanley
1844-1846

46. Robert Garner
Foley
Fenton, Staffordshire
1733-1789

47. Gille Factory
France

48. Wm. Hackwood
Eastwood
Hanley
Stoke-on-Trent, Staffs.
1827-1843

49. Harding & Cotterill
Burton-on-Trent, Staffs.

50. Thomas Harley

Lane End
Staffordshire
1802-1808

51. Wm. Harrop
Hanley, Staffs.

52. Herculaneum Pottery
Liverpool
Lancashire
c1793-1841

53. Joseph Holdcroft
Sutherland Pottery (from c1872)
Staffordshire Potteries (1865-1939)
Restyled Holdcrofts Ltd. (c. 1906)
Longton, Staffs.
1865-1939

54. Hope & Carter
Fountain Place
Burslem, Staffs.
1862-1880

55. Stephen Hughes
Waterloo Road Works
N. Staffordshire
1842-1851

56. Elijah Jones
Villa Pottery
Cobridge, Staffs.
1831-1839

57. George Jones & Sons Ltd.
Trent Pottery
Stoke
1864-1907

58. Jones & Hopkinson
Unknown

59. Jones & Walley
Villa Pottery
Cobridge, Staffs.
1841-1843

60. W.H. Kerr & Co.
Worcester, Worchestershire
1852-1862

61. Wm. Kirkham
London Rd.
Stoke-on-Trent, Staffs.
1862-1892

62. Leveson Hill
Stoke-on-Trent, Staffs.

63. Liddle, Elliot & Son
Dale Hall Pottery
Longport, Staffs.
1862-1871

64. J. & T. Lockett
Staffordshire Potteries
King Street, Longton
1835+

65. Lockett, Baguley & Cooper
Victoria Works
Shelton, Hanley
Staffordshire
1855-1860

66. Machin & Potts
Waterloo Pottery
Burslem, Staffs.
1833-1837

67. J. Macintyre
Burslem, Staffs.

68. Charles James Mason & Co.
Patent Ironstone China
Manufactory Lane Delph, Staffordshire
1829-1845

69. T.J. & J. Mayer
Furlong Works
Dale Hall Pottery
Burslem, Staffordshire
1843-1855

70. Charles Meigh
Old Hall Works
Hanley, Staffs.
1835-1849

71. Charles Meigh, Son & Pankhurst
Old Hall Pottery
Hanley, Staffs.
1850-1851

72. Charles Meigh & Son
Old Hall Pottery
Hanley, Staffs.
1851-1861

73. John Meir & Son
Greengates Pottery
Turnstall, Staffs.

74. Minton
Stoke-on-Trent
Staffs.
1793-present

75. Morley & Ashworth
Broad St.
Hanley, Staffs.
1859-1862

76. J.E. Norton
Bennington, Vermont
USA
1850-1858

77. Old Hall Earthenware Co. Ltd.
Old Hall Pottery
Hanley, Staffs.
1861-1886

78. Pankhurst & Dimmock .
Unknown

79. Phillips & Bagster
High Street
Hanley, Staffs.
1820-1823

80. Pinder, Bourne & Co.
Nile Street
Burslem, Staffs.
1862-1882

81. Pinder, Bourne & Hope
Fountain Place and Nile St.
Burslem, Staffs.
1851-1862

82. Portmeirion Pottery Ltd.
Stoke-on-Trent, Staffs
1962-

83. F. & R. Pratt & Co. Ltd.
High St.
Fenton, Staffs.
1818-

84. Powell & Bishop
Stafford St. Works
Hanley, Staffs.
1876-1878

85. George Ray
Longton and Hanley
c1840-1850

86. E.J. Ridgway
Staffordshire Potteries
Church Works, Hanley
1860+

87. William Ridgway & Co.
Bell Works, Shelton
Church Works, Hanley
Staffordshire Potteries
c1830-1854

88. William Ridgway, Son & Co.
Church Works
Cobden Works
Hanley, Staffs.
c1838-1848
c1841-1846

89. Ridgway & Abington
Church Works
Hanley, Staffs.
c1835-1860

90. J. Roberts
Kent, (Upnor)

91. Rockingham Works
Near Swinton
Yorkshire
1745-1842

92. John Rose & Co.
(Coalport Porcelain Works)
Coalbrookdale, Shropshire
1830-1850

93. Sanford Estate Pottery Clay Co.
Wareham, Dorsetshire
Unknown

94. Sharpe, Brothers & Co.
(Thomas Sharpe)
Swadlincote
Burton-on-Trent
Derbyshire
1821-

95. Schidler & Gerbing
Germany

96. Josiah Spode
Stoke-on-Trent
Staffordshire
1784-1833

97. Thomas Till & Son
Stych Pottery
Burslem, Staffs.
1850-1928

98. John Turner
Lane End
Longton, Staffs.
c1762-1806

99. Edward Walley
Villa Pottery
Cobridge, Staffordshire
1845-1856

100. E. & W. Walley
Cobridge, Staffs.

101. Warburton & Britton
     Leeds
102. Josiah Wedgwood (& Sons Ltd.)
     Burslem
     Etruria
     Barlaston
     c1759-present
     c1759+
     c1769+
     1940-present
103. Wilkinson & Rickhuss
     Hanley, Staffs.
104. Wilkinson & Sons
     Hanley, Staffs.
105. E.A. Wood
     Hanley, Staffs.
106. Enoch & Edward Wood
     Fountain Place
     Burslem, Staffs.
     1818-1846
107. Wood & Brown
     Unknown
108. George Wood & Co.
     Shelton, Staffs.
109. Wood & Sale
     Hanley, Staffs.
110. Worcester
     Kerr & Binns
     Worcester
     1852-1862
111. Worthington & Green
     Brook Street Works
     Shelton, Hanley, Staffs.
     1844-1864
112. Wright & Rigby
     Hanley, Staffs.

Appendix II Glossary of pottery terms

Basalt   A black unglazed stoneware body developed in the 1760s by Josiah Wedgwood. It was very hard and easily moulded which made it suitable for potting both ornamental and teaware articles. Its popularity lasted well into the nineteenth century.

Body   The type of ware from which the piece of pottery is made, i.e. 'Parian' body.

Creamware   A cream colored earthenware body of high quality perfected by Josiah Wedgwood about 1740. It was inexpensive to make, light in weight to ship, and was rarely heavily decorated, which gave it a clean appearance. It became the most popular eighteenth-century body both in England and on the Continent.

Earthenware   A ceramic body made from clay and silica compounds. It is fired at low temperatures and is usually glazed to make it less porous.

Faience   An earthenware body glazed with tin oxide which is opaque and hides the colour of the body.

Glaze   A vitreous substance which covers the surface of the clay to make it smooth, hard and impervious to water.

Intaglio   Any figure engraved or cut into a substance.

Ironstone   An earthenware body patented in 1813 by C.J. Mason which is particularly hard, heavy and durable. It is very similar to stoneware. See stoneware.

Jasperware   A coloured stoneware body, usually unglazed, introduced about 1775 by Josiah Wedgwood. It is close grained and can be highly polished and worked with lapidary's tools. Colour is either on the surface only, called 'dip' jasper, or throughout and called 'solid' jasper.

Kiln   The oven in which pottery is fired.

Lustreware   A method of decorating pottery in which a thin film of metal is deposited on top of the glaze, giving it a shiny surface. The addition of gold results in red, silver in yellow, platinum in silver, and copper in its own colour.

Majolica   A tin-glazed earthenware developed in 1850 by Mintons. It imitated the earlier Maiolica of Italy. In common usage the term means earthenware coloured with semi-translucent glaze.

Parian   A creamy white biscuit porcelain-like body, usually unglazed, made to simulate marble and to be a substitute for the biscuit porcelain of Sèvres. Because it was easily moulded into intricate shapes it was widely used for figures and jugs.

Pearlware Earthenware body introduced by Josiah Wedgwood which is similar to, and often confused with, creamware. Cobalt was added to the glaze for whiteness.

Porcelain A highly refined clay body usually white. It has been fired to a very high temperature which causes it to partly melt and become translucent. A perfect piece will ring when tapped.

Pottery A generic term for anything which has been made of fired clay. In common usage it has come to mean any opaque clay item that has been fired at a lower temperature than that used for stoneware and porcelain.

Press moulding One method for moulding pottery. See page 4, book I for a discussion of this process.

Queen's ware Wedgwood's type of creamware named for Queen Charlotte who ordered a dinner set made from it. See Creamware.

Relief Design on a piece of pottery which rises above the plane surface of the item.

Rosso Antico Josiah Wedgwood's version of red unglazed stoneware, which was copied from the Chinese.

Saggar Fire-proof clay boxes or containers which hold pottery while it is being fired, thus protecting it from the flames and kiln gases. Because the saggars can be stacked, many pieces of pottery can be fired at one time.

Slip Clay diluted with water to a creamy consistency.

Slip cast moulding One method for moulding pottery. See page 4, book I for a discussion of this process.

Smear glaze A glaze for pottery which is very thin with little gloss. Often it was used on the outside of moulded jugs accompanied by a heavy glaze on the inside.

Sprigging Decoration for pottery which is moulded separately from the article and then applied to it.

Stoneware A clay body fired to an extremely high temperature (about 1300°C), which makes it very heavy and hard and impervious to water without the use of a glaze.

Toby Jugs A pottery drinking jug. It usually takes the form of a seated man in a tricorn hat holding a pipe and a mug.

Transfer printing Pottery decoration achieved by pressing soft paper on which an impression has been made from an engraved plate on to the article to be decorated while the oxide-stained oils acting as a kind of ink are still wet. This can be done either overglaze or underglaze.

Vitrify   To convert into glass by heat.

Zaffre   An impure cobalt oxide used to colour blue and white pottery under-glaze. It produced a dark, opaque, cobalt blue.

Appendix III
Additions and Corrections to Book I

Since the publication of *A Collector's Guide to Nineteenth Century Jugs,* a number of unmarked examples have been identified by readers. Also, we have been given additional information and a few corrections on certain jugs. Please note the following:

1. Audrey Dudson has indicated that the following were made by James Dudson:

#71	Chinese Figures
#95	Resting Putti
#143	Stylized Vine (Dudson called this "Vine Leaf")
#144	Sleeping Beauty
#172	Calla Lilly and Wire
#205a	Butter Dish
#205h	Staffordshire Teapot, called "Jewel" by Dudson

2. Corrections and Additions

   #16 Hunt by Minton. A version has been found with a ceramic strainer lid. The pattern number on the bottom changed to #103.

   #21 Winged Lion and Cherubs has been found in white on a buff stoneware body with a ceramic lid. Also, Mr. Paul Fox indicated that this jug should date c1820 instead of c1830.

   #37 Silenus by Minton has been found in terracotta as was the Minton Two Drivers. It would be interesting to know of any other Minton jugs which were potted in a terracotta body.

   #39 Toby Filpot. The two figures on this jug represent Tam O'Shanter and Souter Johnnie.

   #44 The Good Samaritan jug has been found with a bird handle. There is a side view of the bird showing the head, out-stretched wing and body with detailed feathers. We should like to know if anyone else has seen this handle on any other jug.

   #50 "Ranger" was also registered by Samuel Alcock in lavender and white on April 3, 1847.

   #53 Falstaff was also registered by Edward Steel, on November 14, 1882.

   #56 "Portland Vase" was registered by W.T. Copeland on August 17, 1847 under the registration number 45092.

   #64 Fox and Hounds by Minton. The impressed number should read 3952.

   #65 "The Waverly Papers" mark number should read 2690. Also, this pattern has been found in a large dark green mug.

   #70a "Vintage" by Copeland and Garrett. An example has been found in the W.J. Rees collection marked on the base, "Copeland and Garretts," (note the 's' on Garretts) and titled "Beauvais Jug." There is an impressed 18.

   #71 Chinese Figures. A marked example has been found impressed: S. Hughes & Co.

#75   "Hops" by Minton has been found with a blue background with white moldings and in white parian with a ceramic (parian) lid.

#76   Bullrushes has been found in dark blue with white cattails.

#81   "Sylvan" has been found in white parian with green enamelled ivy and red berries.

#89   Cain and Abel was also made by Thomas Till and Son in bright green and white and registered on June 3, 1854.

#90   "Aristo" should read "Ariosto." "Tasso and Ariosto." This jug was also made by Bradbury, Anderson and Bettanny.

#95   Resting Putti has been found with a pink background.

#96   Storks Among the Grapes has been found with a pink background.

#102   Putti and Grapes. The 1851 catalog for the Crystal Palace Exhibition shows a drawing of this jug and credits it to Charles Meigh. Also an eight inch example has been found marked Worthington and Green.

#108   The Dancers. The dancing figures on this jug have been identified by the Museum of Theatre as Grisi and Perrot dancing the opera polka.

#120   The Wedding. This jug, which I have called The Wedding, has been found with "Dunmow" impressed on the bottom. A collector has suggested that this probably indicates that the procession is not a wedding procession, but rather is an illustration of the Dunmow Flitch, a traditional custom involving the awarding of a side of bacon (the flitch) to the married couples who were able to swear that they never had a cross word during the past year. A judge was appointed to determine the veracity of the couples. There obviously would have been a procession of the couples who participated as illustrated on this jug #120. This information would also call into question the naming of jug #35, book I, potted by Minton, as the design would seem to be the same. You may want to change the name of both of these jugs in your records.

#124   Grape Vine has been found in blue and white. Also, the blue pattern mark should read 51.

#125   "Cup Tosser" has been found made of earthenware and marked Cork and Edge.

#128   "Ino." This jug was exhibited in 1855 in the Paris Exhibition. It was also made by E. Walley.

#140   Scrolls and Flowers. Brownfield named this jug "Eglantine."

#146   Ridgway's Chrysanthemum has been found with an impressed "Flora" on the bottom.

#149   Water lilies. Alcock also made a version of this jug with a slightly different neck.

#170   Brownfield's "Tiverton" jug has been found with a wine background and white flowers.

#192   "Garibaldi." An example has been found in the W.J. Rees collection marked Cork & Edge. Cork and Edge became Cork, Edge and Malkin in 1860, so the old mark, Cork & Edge, must have been used here. An example of this jug has been found in white on lavendar ground marked Copestake Bros., Longton.

#204c   A reader has made an interesting query concerning "c" under 204, Book I, additional designs, which was called Julius Caesar. He questions that the head, though Roman or classical in look, is in fact Julius Caesar, and questions that England would be honoring Caesar at this time. 1853 is the date that England was honoring the death of Wellington. We may well stand corrected.

NOTE: We invite all readers to send any other additions or corrections which you have in your possession to:
Kathy Hughes
Tudor House Galleries
1401 East Blvd.
Charlotte, N.C. 28203
U.S.A.

Bibliography

Art Journal Illustrated Catalogue of the Great Exhibition 1851 and 1862.

Art Journal Illustrated Catalogue of the Universal Exhibition 1867.

Atterbury, J., *European Pottery and Porcelain*, Mayflower Books, 1979.

Barret, Richard Carter, *Bennington Pottery and Porcelain*, Bonanza, 1958.

Barret, Richard Carter, *How to Identify Bennington Pottery*, Stephen Green Press, 1964.

Bodey, Hugh, *Twenty Centuries of British Industry*, David & Charles, 1975.

City Museum, Stoke on Trent, *Stonewares and Stonechinas of Northern England, to 1851*, City Museum, 1982.

Colliers Encyclopedia, P.F. Collier & Son, 1950.

Cushion, J.P., *Pocket Book of British Ceramic Marks*, Faber & Faber, 1959.

Durant, Will and Ariel, *Rousseau and Revolution*, Simon & Schuster, 1967.

Godden, Geoffrey A., Encyclopedia of British Pottery and Porcelain Marks, Bonanza, 1964.

Godden, Geoffrey A., *An Illustrated Encyclopedia of British Pottery and Porcelain*, Bonanza, 1965.

Godden, Geoffrey A., *The Illustrated Guide to Ridgway Porcelain*, Barrie & Jenkins, 1972.

Godden, Geoffrey A., *Jewitt's Ceramic Art of Great Britain 1800-1900*, Barrie & Jenkins, 1972.

Godden, Geoffrey A., *British Pottery. An Illustrated Guide*, Barrie & Jenkins, 1974.

Godden, Geoffrey A., Godden's Guide to Mason's China and the Ironstone Wares, Antique Collector's Club, 1980.

Haggar, R.G., Mountford, A.R., and Thomas, J. *'Pottery' in Victoria County History of Staffordshire*, vol. 2, Oxford University Press, 1967.

Henrywood, R.K., 'The Moulded Jugs of William Ridgway and His Successors,' and 'The Moulded Jugs of William Brownfield,'' *Antique Collecting Magazine*.

Henrywood, R.K., *Relief Moulded Jugs, 1820-1900*, Antique Collector's Club Ltd., 1984.

May, John and Jennifer, *Commemorative Pottery*, Heinemann, 1972.

Paton, James, *Jugs. A Collectors' Guide*, Souvenir Press, 1976.

Public Records Office, Kew, for registration of designs.

Scriven, Samuel, Esq., evidence given to the Children's Employment Commission, *Appendix to the Second Report of the Commissioners, Traders and Manufacturers*, Vol. 2, *Reports and Evidence from Sub-Commissioners*, London, 1842.

Shinn, Charles and Dorrie, *Victorian Parian China*, Barrie & Jenkins, 1971.

Smith, Alan, *The Illustrated Guide to Herculaneum 1796-1840,* Barrie & Jenkins, 1970.

Wakefield, Hugh, *Victorian Pottery,* Barrie & Jenkins, 1962.

Index by Jug Title

Index by Potter